GW01367519

# DUB'S PUBS

*The definitive guide to Dublin's finest*

## DJ DORAN

*read electric*
DUBLIN

*Dub's Pubs*
Written by DJ Doran
Photography by J. Farrell & DJ Doran
Cover shot by W. Werbel
Illustration by L. Schultz

First Edition
Published July 2005
by **Read Electric**

ISBN 0-9550492-0-2

Copyright © DJ Doran 2005

The right of DJ Doran to be identified as the author of this work
has been asserted by him in accordance with the
Copyright, Designs and Patents Act 1988.

All rights reserved. No part of this publication may be reproduced,
stored in or introduced into a retrieval system,
or transmitted, in any form, or by any means (electronic,
mechanical, photocopying, recording or otherwise) without the prior
written permission of the publisher. Any person who does any unauthorized
act in relation to this publication may be liable to criminal prosecution and
civil claims for damages.

First Edition

A CIP Catalogue record for this book is available from the British Library.

Typesetting and Design by **Read Electric**,
Suite 8, 184 Lower Rathmines Road, Dublin 6, Ireland
www.readelectriconline.com
readelectriconline@hotmail.com

Graphic Design by Digiprint.ie, 53 Rathgar Avenue, Dublin 6

This book is made in Ireland

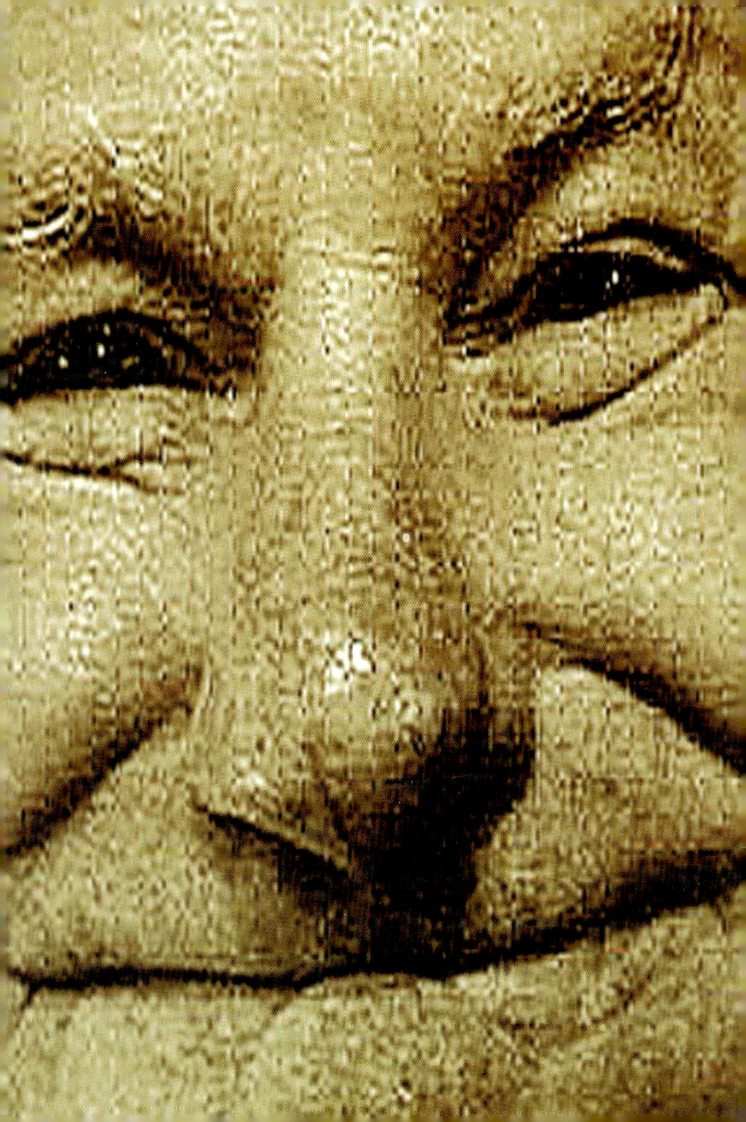

# Preface

Dublin! Oh, Dublin! Mystical and ancient jewel cast carelessly aside and found anew! Such depth! Such worned lines! A lifetime of pain and joy time-scarred onto every grey façade without shame or pretext. A living face!

Dublin's lack of spectacular monuments (the type of which you can tick off in your convenient little book) is more than adequately substituted for by a far more meaningful, artful and unmistakable force – *yes, that's right* – her pubs. The lifeblood of this ever-evolving city – eight hundred (and counting) very different but absolutely essential cells, clamouring collectively as the true heartbeat – birthing inspiration, celebration, revelation, salivation.

Yes, every up and down of city life is here, on display somewhere in a Dublin pub. Find it, observe it, embrace it – be a part of its soul – and when you know it, you will know this place and you will see why it has been constantly replicated (in theory) across the globe. And why? *Spirit*! Not booze, food, music or décor. Spirit and plain old honest character.

The haunt of literary giants,
The other woman in a million marriages,
The social hub of generations,
The place for good and bad news,
The spawning ground of countless love-stories,

The friend to many,
A comfort to all,
A psychiatrist,
A priest,
A counsellor,
A business partner,

A mutual philosopher,
A muse beyond muses whatever the hour,
A sympathiser,
A lover,
A legend,
A pub.

It can be whatever you want it to be or it can be nothing. Go on – stay at home or in your hotel, trembling knock-kneed before your mini-bar, and pretend you're not in one of the world's most vibrant cities – there'll be all the more for the rest of us!

*

In this first edition of Dub's Pubs, I will take you to sixty-nine of Dublin's finest. Not necessarily the biggest, brightest, coolest, oldest, far-famed, cheapest, shiniest or safest (or any of that anaesthetised guide book rubbish) but sixty-nine that I would actually use. And do.

A personal companion from a Dublin perspective. It doesn't get more accurate or, indeed, honest. In fact, half the fun of pubbing it in Dublin is finding one for yourself that suits. So after you've read this weighty tome, then put it away and let your feet do the talking. Get out there, find a piece for yourself and squander it selfishly. I mean, don't even stay city centre if you don't want. There are plenty of cracking pubs beyond the canals and further and sincere apologies to those we couldn't include this time. So come on! Pass on the word to your loved ones and join us in celebration of the greatest alehouses on the planet.

Comment, additions, offers of drink or proposals of marriage to: <u>readelectriconline@hotmail.com</u>

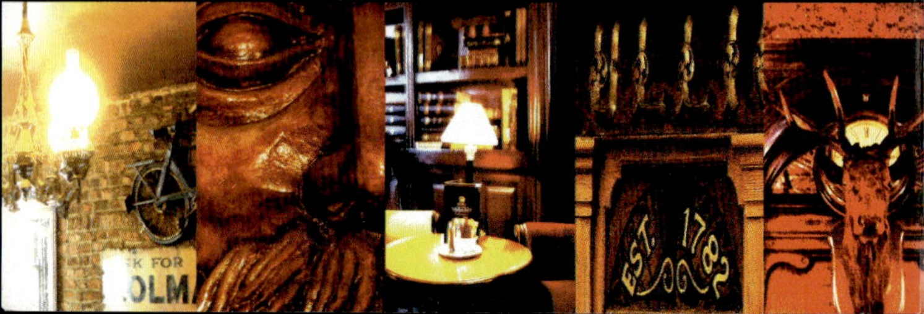
EST. 1782

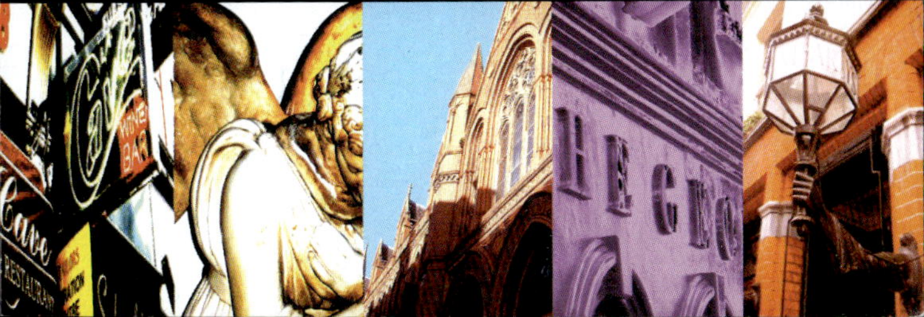
WINE BAR
Cave

BIG TREE TAVERN

# The Big Tree
## Dorset Street Lower

**1**

No, not the Northside's shrine to the Blessed Trinity, or indeed Man Utd, Liverpool and Arsenal (though these would be closer), but in a far more matter-of-fact way, though not too surprisingly, this house stands in tribute to a dirty great tree. Now, unfortunately no longer with us I would like to think that the mighty branches have lived on in the creation of The Big Tree's updownandtotheside bar arrangement which can take some traversing on a busy day. Nevertheless, in this area there are a mixture of pubs employing a mixture of standards (that's being kind) and The Tree stands proudly at the top end of the field. And speaking of fields, if you're heading to Croke Park, be sure to water down here before or after to savour the hectic anticipation and/or big match critique from a hundred barstool pundits.

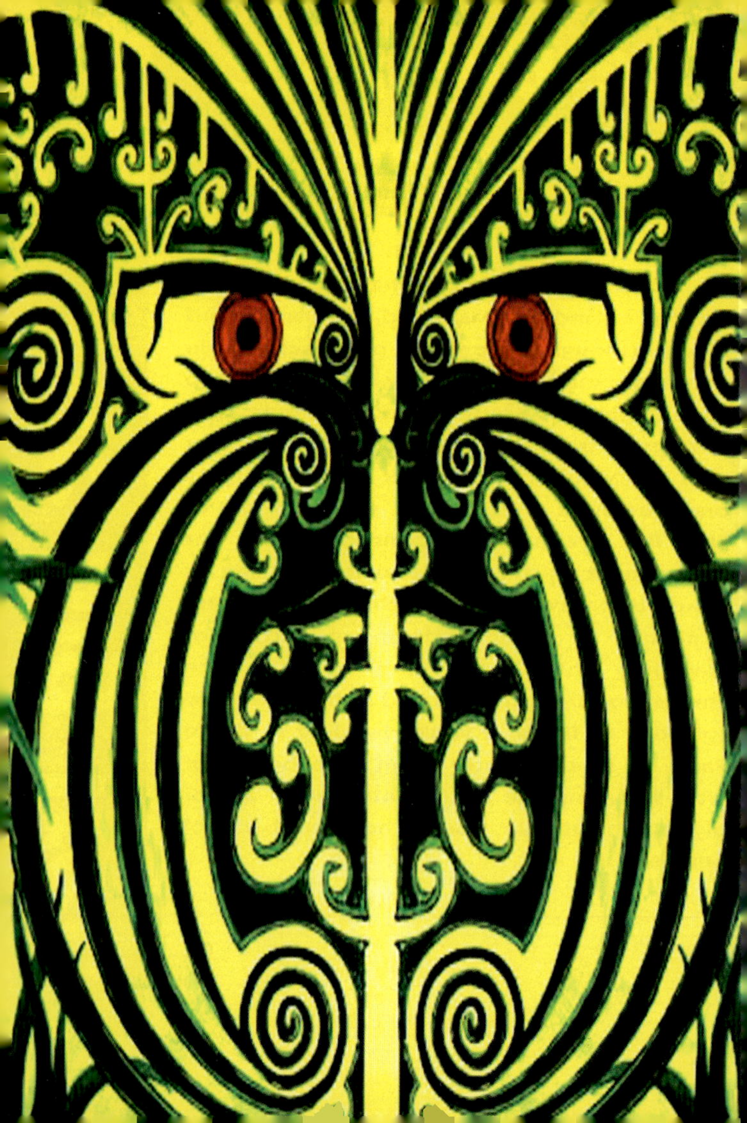

# The Woolshed
## Parnell Street

**2**

In an instant karma kind of way, for all the *bad* Oirish bars that claim to *exist* far and wide across the globe, finally, a themed bar that remains true to form, in the heart of Dublin of all places! Anyone who has seen the vast array of urban bars in Oz or NZ will immediately recognise something familiar here; ie: standing (for real blokes), sports, sports, sports and as much VB or Speight's you can fit down your gullet before falling over. Okay, a generalisation, I accept, but this is where the Southern Hemisphere cats choose to meet and, you know, it makes a nice change from bar/lounge/snug proliferations. Top tucker, and comfortable booths make this an ideal spot for a pre or post movie swift one and has a genuinely relaxed and homely vibe - if a little rowdy, at times. The Woolshed is definitely one of the best value pinthouses in town and, more tremendously, IT HAS A POOL TABLE, which poolheads will tell you, is few and far between these days. Oh yes.

70. PATRICK CONWAY.

# Patrick Conway's
## Parnell Street

**3**

Now, when a pub advertises itself as a lounge, that does not necessarily mean any guarantees of comfort. This place has to be the exception to the power of ten. This is comfort personified. The kind of luxurious interior you'd easily fall in love with (if you were that way inclined – or reclined for that matter) having trawled the usual sub-standard loungery offered elsewhere. I mean, even the bar is comfortable. It's just great here to while away a few hours and the deep carpet, lazy seats, soft lighting and array of pictures are so homely it would be a work of business genius were it contrived – but you just know it isn't. After a long, hard day at the grindstone, all you want to do is go home and relax and shut out the harsh lashings of the day. Well, now you don't have to! Just come here! I'm not sure if they'd let you slouch about in your dressing gown and bunny slippers, but beyond that, I'd say anything goes. They are so considerate here, they even supply a huge wonderful clock which means you don't need to strain or slit your tired eyes to see when it's time to go. Such profound altruism. I nominate Conway's for the Nobel Pub Prize.

**Patrick Conway's**

72

# Parnell Mooney
## Parnell Street

**4**

Long and far-famed as the traditional *waiting room* for expectant Dublin fathers in which they could *do their* bit while the missus sweated it out over the road, (or the other way round where ghost pregnancies are concerned – think Charles Hawtrey in Carry On Doctor), the Parnell Mooney was always a popular and comfortable city lounge familiar to the rich and poor of generations. Whether pre-bus or post-hospital, it was always a safe bet in an otherwise decaying area – a landmark, if you like. *If you can feel a 'but' coming on, you're right..* For progress is fine, sometimes essential, and improvement, the same. But to take out a diamond and replace it with perspex is just a real pity – something I can never quite get my head around. Now obviously here, they are trying to catch the affluent young crowd and, fair play to them, they have cash to burn. But surely making someone stay all day or night is a much more lucrative prospect than in and out on a fast-food counter, wipe you down and see you next Friday. Still, Parnell Mooney is the best example of an outer city lounge in the city centre.

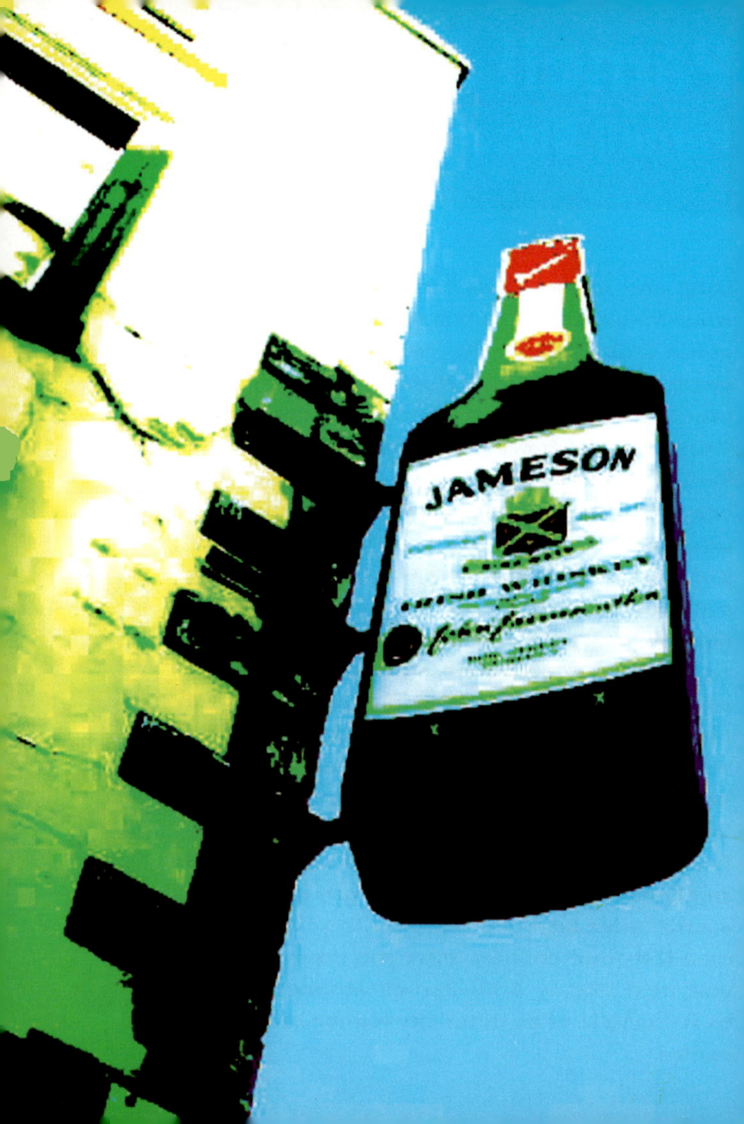
JAMESON

# Flowing Tide
## Lower Abbey Street

**5**

This two-part popular watering hole houses the ying and yang of Dublin pub life. Upstairs, theatreland's haven, traders' wharf and shoppers' oasis, where an older crowd of regulars, actors, play-actors and irregulars, frequent the comfortable furnishings, and downstairs, darker, deeper, lively, loud and studenty. Under the Tide, (as one might, classically, expect), you find the Neptune and as well-known a rock'n'roll nightspot you are unlikely to find this side of the Liffey. Unchanged for years, it is this very reliability that makes The Flowing Tide such an enduring favourite between locals and visitors alike. This basement is a rumbustuous but hearty contender for hideaway of the year and sheltered from the responsible rays of daylight, you could squander many an afternoon gently flowing here, rolling inevitably into an energetic and wild-eyed evening.

78 THE OVAL 78

# The Oval
## Middle Abbey Street

**6**

I remember vividly, the very first time I sat in The Oval. It would have been mid-afternoon, about ten years ago, and I sat by the window listening to the bells of Dublin, staring wistfully (semi-drunkenly) out onto Middle Abbey Street's rooftops. I was shaken out of my trance by an overheard snarl between barman and haggard customer. *That's all we need! Another derelict writer.* Had I realised they were referring to me, I might have been flattered though a little confused, for if The Oval is not an ideal place for writers (whether derelict or not) then I don't know where is. The defining factor, is in positioning, of course. A daily local to traders, journos, legal eagles, shoppers, bookheads, historians, daydreamers, the jaded and the faded. A democracy of a pub! All walks of life. Sit up on the first-floor balcony and observe the natural synthesis of daily Dublin or coalesce down by the windowed harp and draw out the ancient grain that is prelude to daydream.

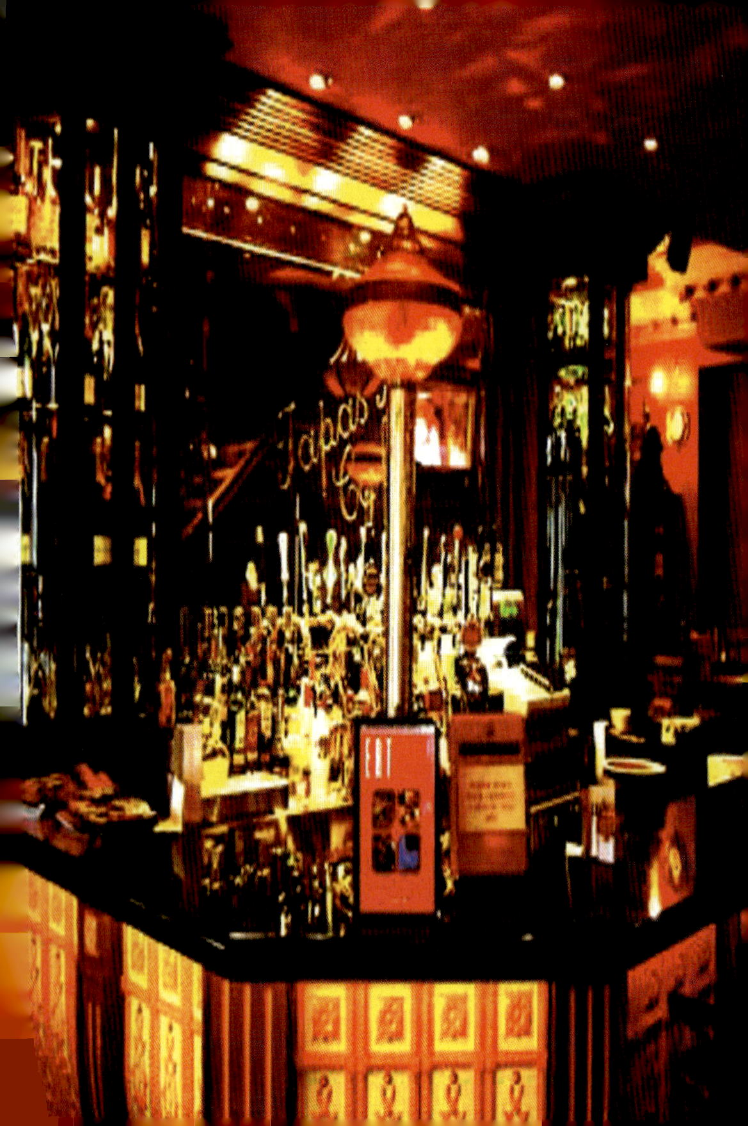
Tapas
EAT

# Gin Palace
## Middle Abbey Street

**7**

The sign of a good pub to me, is one which, in passing, makes you think, *Mmmm! I'd love to partake in a liquid refreshment of sorts within that establishment.* It was cold, it was raining – unusual for Dublin – and that is exactly what I thought and, consequently did. Into the gaslamp and mirrored, Victorian interior, up onto the deep red leatherette – a true Dub Pub – a last bastion of days gone by, when boozers were designed ornately but to last. Reminded me, immediately, of the Princess Louise in Holborn – one of London's classic gin palaces. Estimating at least 105 years in age, I spluttered unbelievably (but tastefully) when the barman told me it was barely 1 year old. So, there you go – shows you how much I know about interior design. And if you are bored enough, or interested, on close inspection the fittings here are actually quite a mixture (though, seemingly of the period) which just add to this pub's warmly individual streak. The other half of this bar appears to have been transmitted directly from Barcelona.

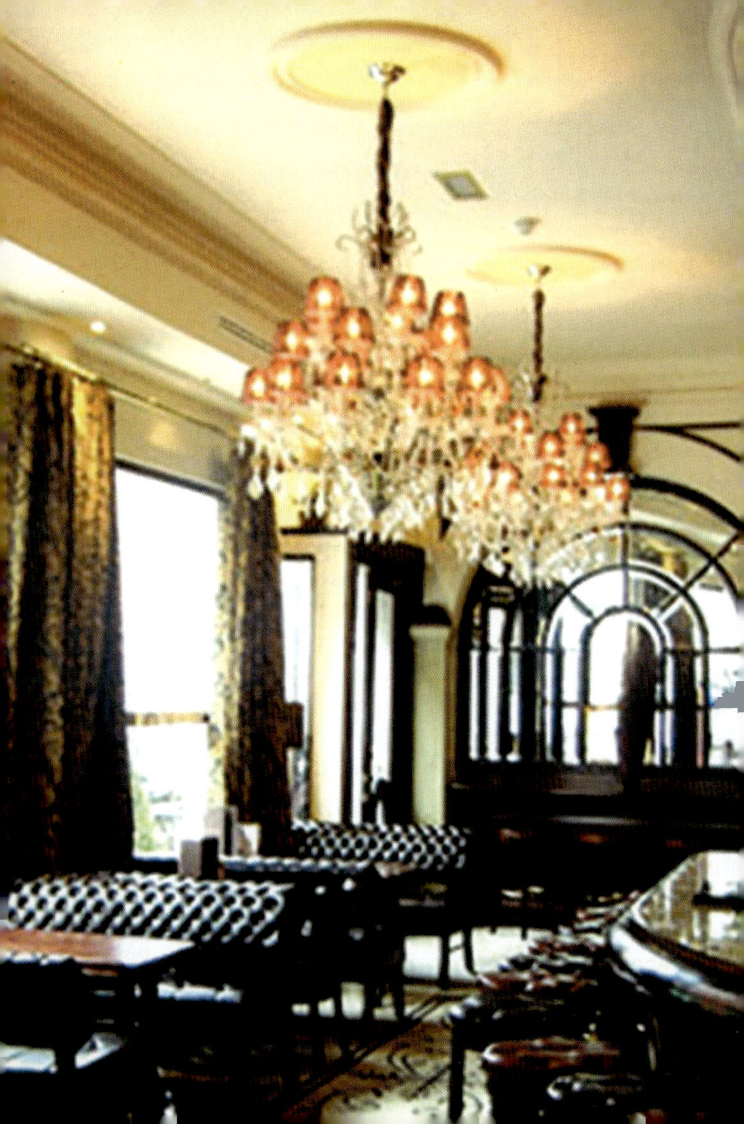

# The Lotts
**Lotts**

**8**

This is a fantastically bizarre find. Part Marseille grand café, part St-Lazare restaurant and all within a miniscule trot from the Ha'penny Bridge. Unlikely? Absolutely! But, you know, who needs sentimental auld Paris when you can have spirited, sexy Dublin. A description that simply would never have been uttered fifteen years ago, surrounding the kind of bar that just would not have worked. Unlike many of the grander bars and pseudo-grand bars springing up, there is a friendly and comfortable air amongst the chandeliers and mirrors here and there is something indefinably calming. Maybe it's because The Lotts does not pretend to be something it's not, (which the sensitive Dub would object to, no doubt), but cheerily adorns its façade in tasteful and warm humour. I can imagine myself sat here on a black Dublin winter evening, heartwarming whiskey in hand, being serenaded by the gorgeous grand piano, dreaming of the seafront stroll in sweltering Marseille and whether the punters there are sat in some Dalkey Archive pub, wistfully lamenting dear Dublin and its gentle rain. Ah, the irony of it all.

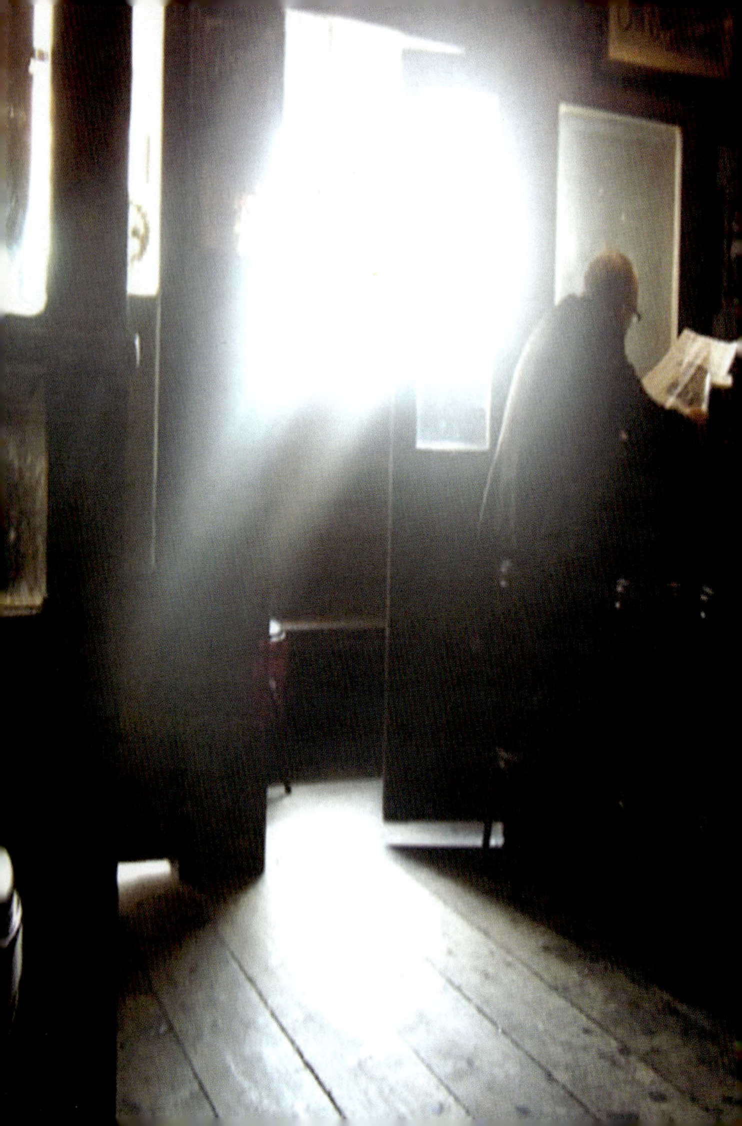

# Kiely's
## Abbey Street Upper

**9**

If you woke up at the bar here from some deep coma-like daydream, then you might be forgiven for thinking the last seventy years had never happened. Not for one second taking anything away from Kiely's — in fact, on the contrary, this is one of the old school — and, in that, one of the best. Dark, shadowy wood and confessional snug — one pure inch of dust on the shelves behind the bar. Old medals, old packs of Navy Cut, aged and ancient bottles — a visual CV of the purest experience. Why, then, do places like this put up televisions? The pub was and should always be the haven of hushed or vocal conversation. If a news matter is that significant, then it will arrive in good time. The auld ghosts, here, have enough to put up with listening to the pseudo-intellectual mickey mouse nonsense coming from one-spritzer-too-many hacks who should have something better to talk about — or be doing, for that matter. Nevertheless, from the shopping hell and purchase panic, this is what escape is all about. Now, back to my coma...

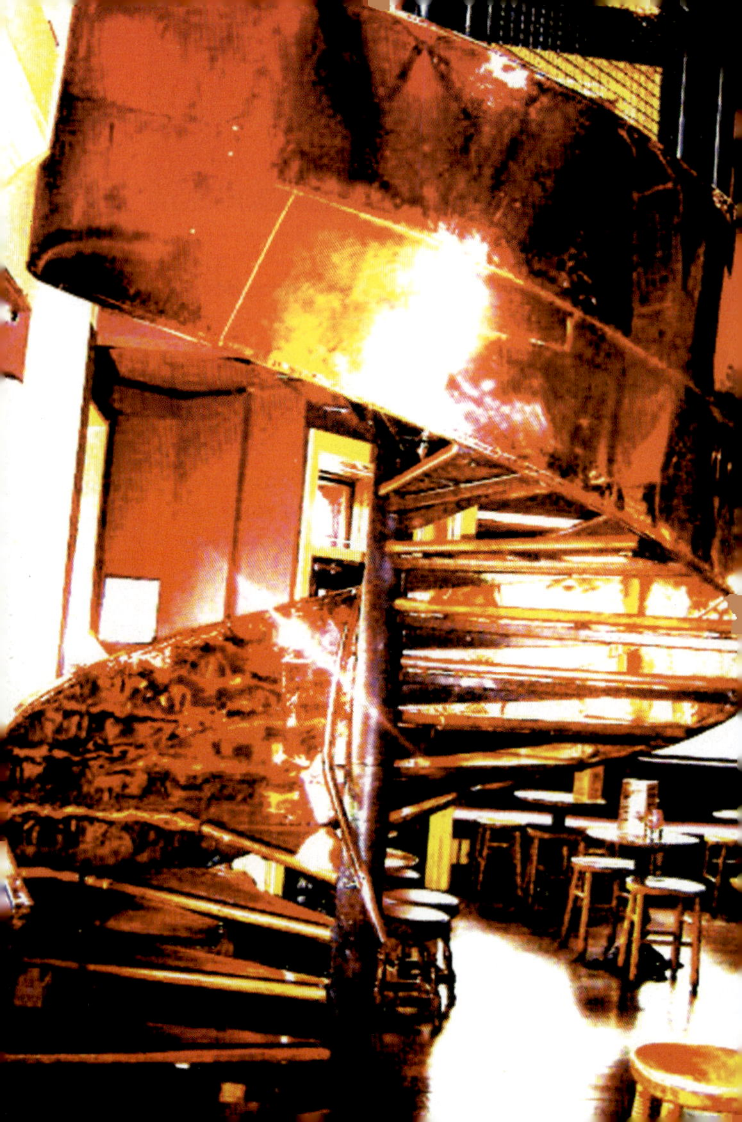

# T.P. Smith's
## Jervis Street

**10**

If, by any chance, you suffer from an acute phobia of spending your valuable Sunday afternoon being dragged around shopping centres looking at curtains, shoes and other items of nonsensical potential spouse purchase, then let me tell you about the solution. Firstly, create a fictional name, (one he/she will not know), and holler it across the chrome mall as loud as you can, whilst speeding in the direction of Smith's, explaining convincingly that said person is your bestest friend of all-time who owes you fifty euros. With that door shut, open up into the warmth and convivial environs of one of the nicest North City bars and chill-out at the marble bar. Ignore the guilty expression on your face and watch as it changes to a lasting inane grin of temperance in the copper-surround reflection. Relax in the studio-loft first floor lounge and take in the bird's eye view of the surrounding mayhem outside, forgetting innocently, the tempest that is approaching and will surely swallow you up. That's right, deal with that later.

SLATTERY

BUDWEISER

# Slattery's
## Capel Street

**11**

Once the bastion of blistering rock and roll, spit and sawdust mayhem and dark hole music scene roughage, I was left (for once) speechless at the complete transformation of this place. In fact, I had to ask was it the very same dank, slightly intimidating, wonder that for many years was *the* best live music venue in Dublin. *One and the same* apparently, but in location only. For you see, the Slattery's of old has changed utterly and inevitably evolved into something certainly *other* than premium locale for putting the musty world to right over a few dusty, philosophical cool ones. In fact, you'd probably be best leaving the auld flatcap at home. But regardless of the author's romantic notions, this place regularly and rumbustuously jumps (particularly on the weekend) and is a definite highlight of the chrysalis Capel Street. The interior is sleek with a *different* menu but you can't help but sense a prim vibe here. Almost fragile. With a little bit more wear and tear and a soupçon of this pub's older, truer self, the results could well be interesting.

*Slattery's*

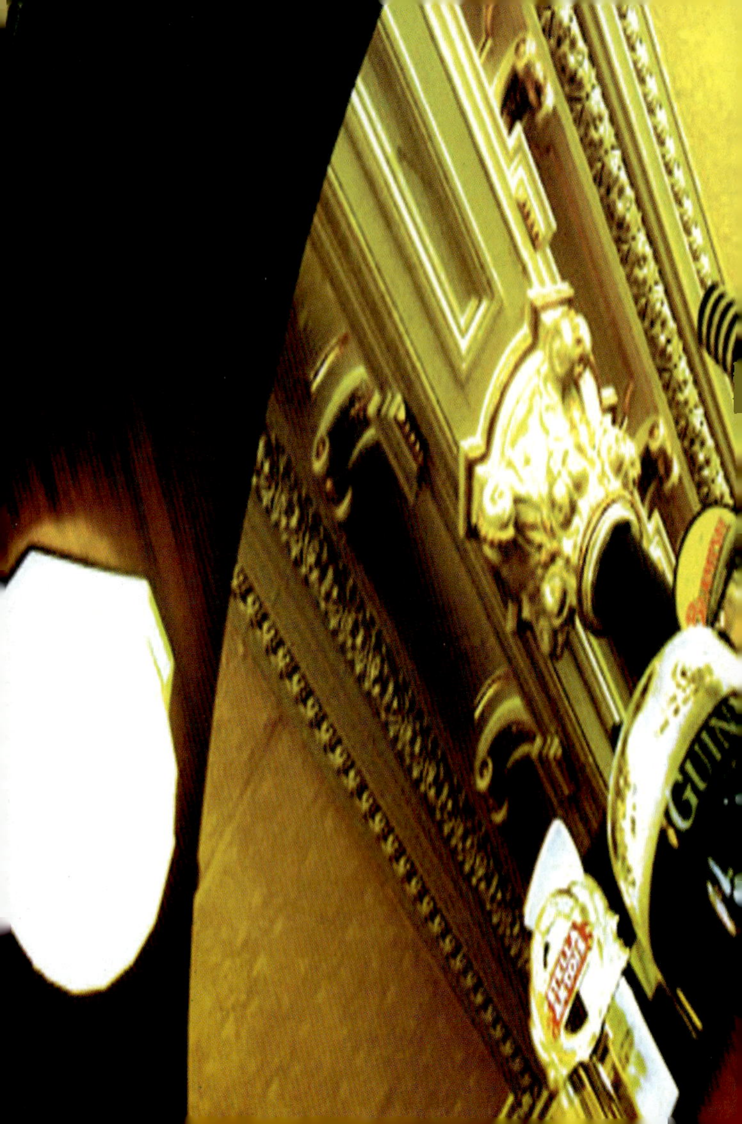

# Jack Nealon's
## Capel Street

**12**

It seems to me, that the whole Capel Street to Smithfield area is one permanent bomb site at the moment with constant excavations, renovations and obliterations. None of which offer any rational reason to want to be here on a rainy winter night, until that is, you pass the warm *real fire* glow of Nealon's and feel the redeeming pull of this much-loved shelter. As unpretentious as it gets, Jack's is probably the most tastefully lit pub in Dublin and though, essentially, just a room, a wooden bar and a fire, it has sackloads of taste and character written all over its face. Now, scholars of pub design might notice a change in the Nealon's of 30 years ago – but so what? It's respectful and totally in tune with reality, without losing any of its former grace. And the moral of the story is? Well – pub designers and they who will desecrate, look first on how it should be done and where it actually works. Look at Jack Nealon's.

# Sin É
## Ormond Quay Upper

**13**

In every few years, all the mystical stars line up and create moments of myth and/or mayhem. If you are fortunate, their consequences concur in your own backyard and you are blessed with the opportunity of experiencing something truly spectacular and, in exceptional circumstances, unifying. Okay! Back to earth! This is only a lowly bar after all - but mein Gott, what a bar! I think there is a very good chance that this place is **THE THRESHOLD**. A peephole into a sunnier dimension where ray upon ray of brilliant light streams inspired from the perfect music collection given out effortlessly from within these walls. This is not an exaggeration. The word is out and the word is correct. This *is* it, indeed! Day and night, Johnny Cash, Otis Redding, Lou Reed, manic jazz, Lennon, La's, Marley. Full-blown Bowie singalongs at 1 o'clock in the afternoon! Talk about a star in it's ascendency? You wouldn't even be close! Brilliantly unpredictable and masterfully cool about it.

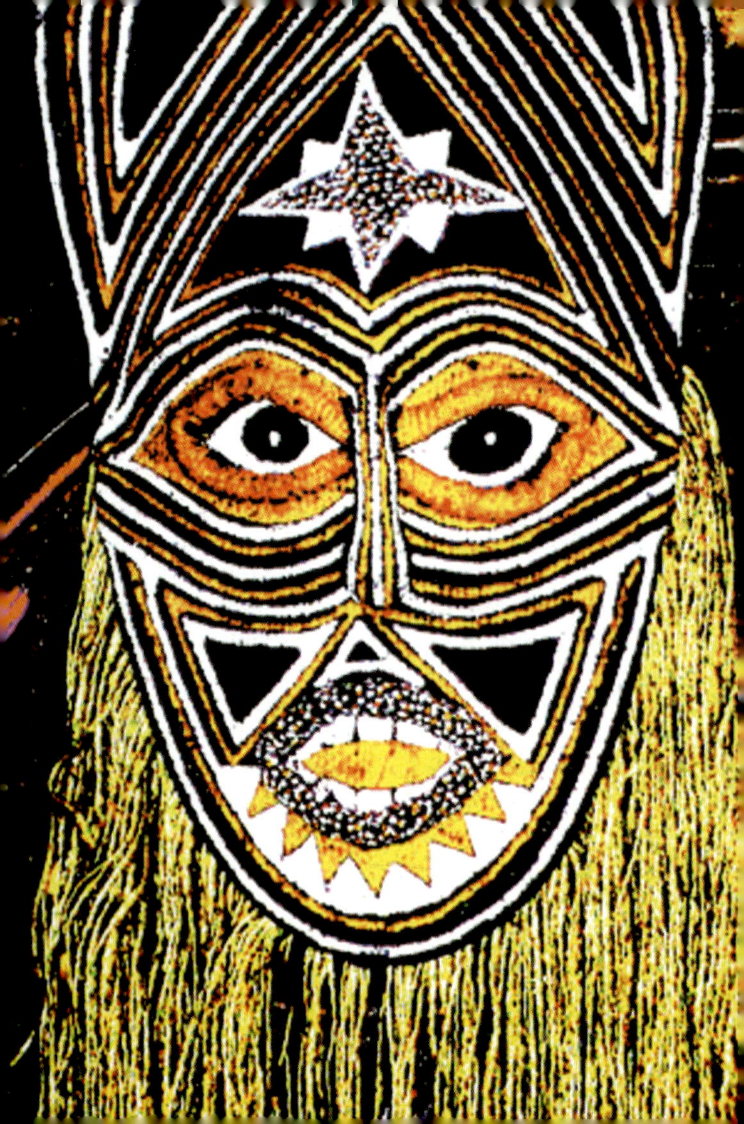

# Voodoo Lounge
## Arran Quay

**14**

In the burgeoning and brilliant Dublin music scene, there are three bars that are streaking ahead in the stakes for best respected venues – in the eyes of musicians and fans. They are, (in any order you like), Whelan's, Eamon Doran's and Voodoo. If it's the best of live music you're after, then go to one of these – there's no two ways about it. What Voodoo has, better than the others though, is a damn cool bar with a great chilled-out vibe. I mean, who doesn't like the shadows flung off soft candlelight as a precursor to intrigue, general effulgence or romance? This is the kind of place you can just as comfortably hang-out at the New York bar, as stare wistfully into the eyes of your beau, planning some classic affair, before having it all shattered by the cold Liffey walk back into town. Thank God for taxis! It's only a matter of time before this place becomes colossal so get down to where the young dudes are now. The *real* dudes in this town. P.S. Dear Huey, a few couches out back wouldn't hurt.

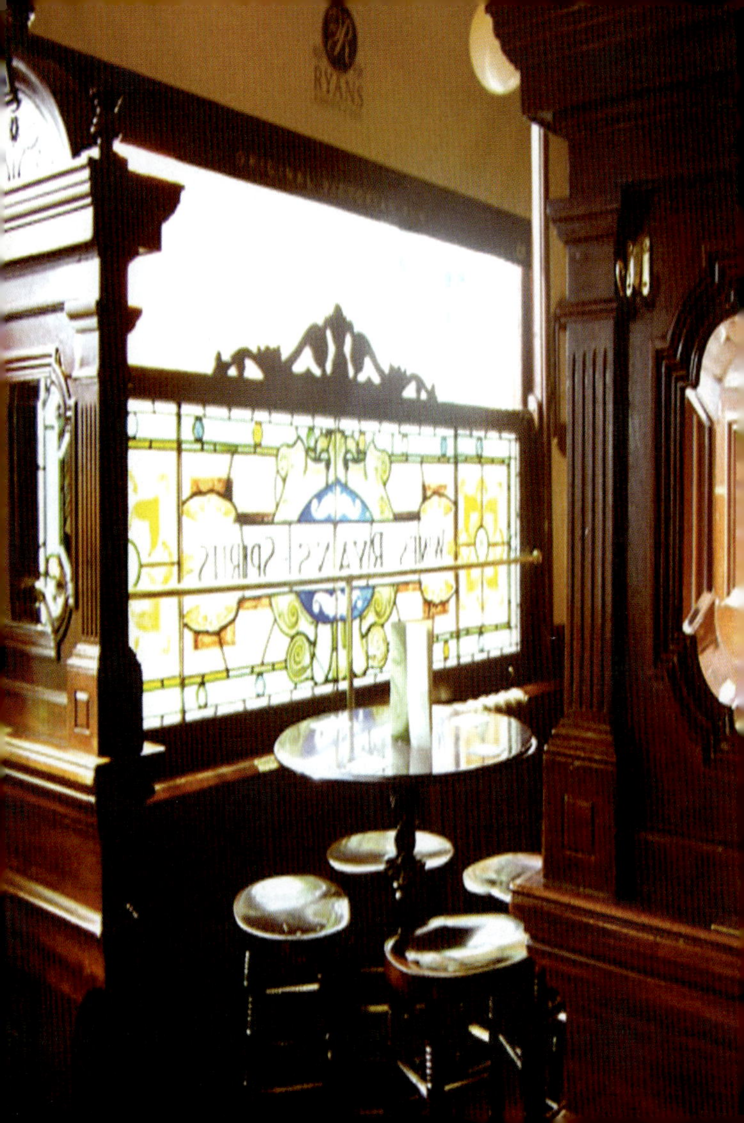
RYANS

# Ryan's
## Parkgate Street

**15**

Pubs come and go, styles change, customers move on. But at the core of all of this, is the underlying purpose of the pub. A place to relax, to commune - an escape hatch of sorts. And as an escape hatch from the unforgiving river winds sending the blueness up your kilt, Ryan's is a utopian spot. It reminded me of a Victorian summer-house, all proper and refined. That would probably be a *light* thing. It is very bright inside, magnified tenfold by the beautiful old mirrors. You won't fall asleep in here! And I doubt they ever see any shenanigans of that sort, being a gentleperson's place. In this day and age of *dubious* standards, gangs of bouncers, beery monsters, etc., a bit of excellence really goes down well. In fact, the staff here were genuine and professional without licking any boots and convinced me to stay for four when I only meant to stay for one. Give those gents a payrise! Professionally run, professionally laid-out, peaceful and classy. I will be back. Simple as that.

# G.F. HANDEL

# G.F. Handel's
## Thomas Court

**16**

To one untrained in the art of pub-crawlery, or one adverse to the typical Liberties house of refreshment, you might stumble upon Handel's and cry out, *HALLELUJAH!* (sorry - Ed.) or some other classically-inspired paean, in the belief that you found a saviour in imbibitionary terms. And to be brutally honest, you would be more than correct. For there are droves of dungeons in this locale and Handel's stands out like a beckoning light amid them. Now, I'm not sure, I might have got this completely wrong, but I really got a Gothic church feel to this pub, (which is extremely appropriate being in the Christchurch vicinity), and could imagine a pipe-organist wurlitzing out some deathly chant in the far corner. Okay, I accept it! The absinthe has to stop, but you will agree that here is contemplative. One side reminded me of a choir's knave from some grand cathedral and at the opposite end were two great candles, cascading white wax into Madonna shapes. Spooky? Yes, a bit. Atmospheric is the word. Can *you* name a church where they serve Guinness? There you go then.

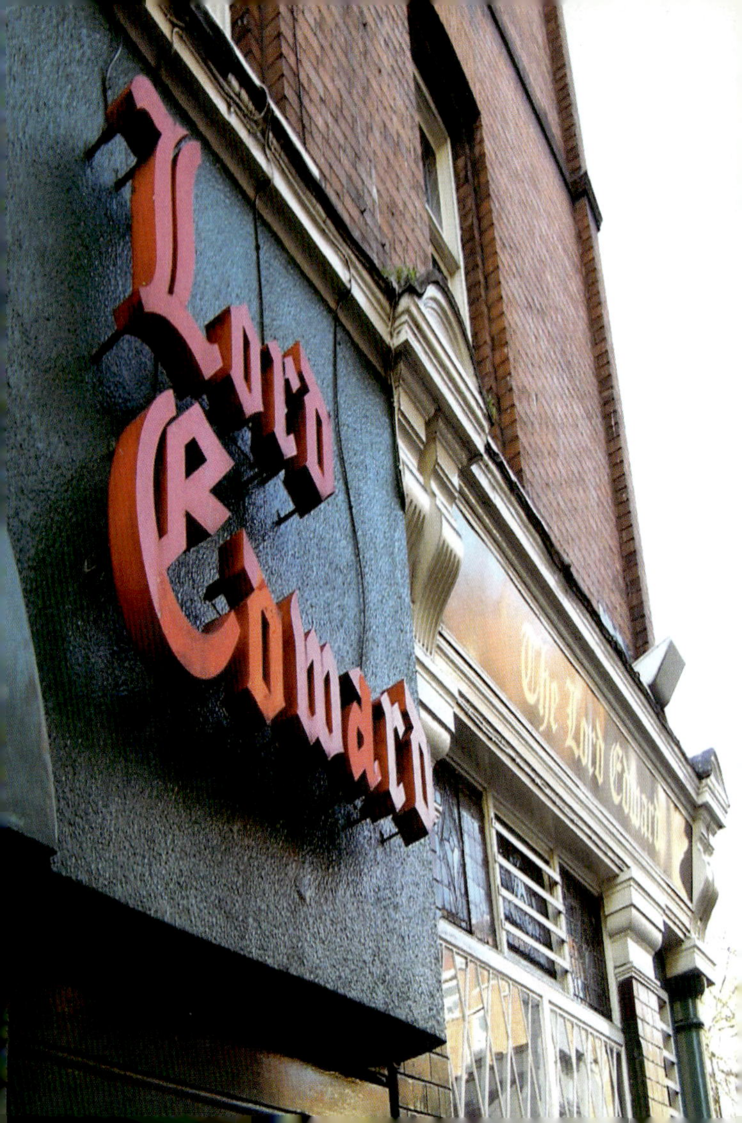

Lord Edward
The Lord Edward

# Lord Edward
## Christchurch Place

**17**

Oh the things these walls have seen! Men with beards and elastic slacks! Smoked-glass conversations traded randomly across the counter! Flickering flame giggling quietly in the corner! The bold and boisterous held in session by omnipresent landlord! What a living vision of the past, of Dublin long-gone! But also of her present! Of the remainder of the less cynical/disrespectful/greedy days and of the elements that cannot and do not wish to or need to join the maniacal charge to oblivion. So here an honest, autumnal affair, where serenity is there for the taking (should it be required), or an insight into the wisecracking wisdom of a dying breed. And all timed to perfection by the constant and reminiscent ringing bells of Christchurch. There aren't many places left like The Lord Edward, particularly in the city centre, so we are very fortunate that it remains fastidious and nonchalant in it's lack of desire to follow the soulless herd.

# The Brazen Head

**Ireland's Oldest Pub**
**ESTD. 1198**

# Brazen Head
## Lower Bridge Street

**18**

Amongst all the hullabaloo of the modern Dublin, the traffic, whirring of cranes, wailing of sirens, there stands an ornate and ancient travellers' rest. Roll up the rickety cart and water the horse in the shadows of Guinness' chimneys and regress somewhat to the candlelit conspiratorial nights of Emmet and his United Irishmen, hatching their doomed revolt by the fireplace. This is best imagined on a dark, wintry evening, when only the hardy are abroad and the suits and chattering Mediterranean students are shored up under duvets and manifold TV dinners. You can hear the hooves and distant shouts, barely audible over the swirling swells!... Right, that's it. I am drinking only water from now on. Linger in the courtyard on balmy summer evenings (there are usually two per year) and appreciate the ancient, yet alive, in the midst of rigorous change.

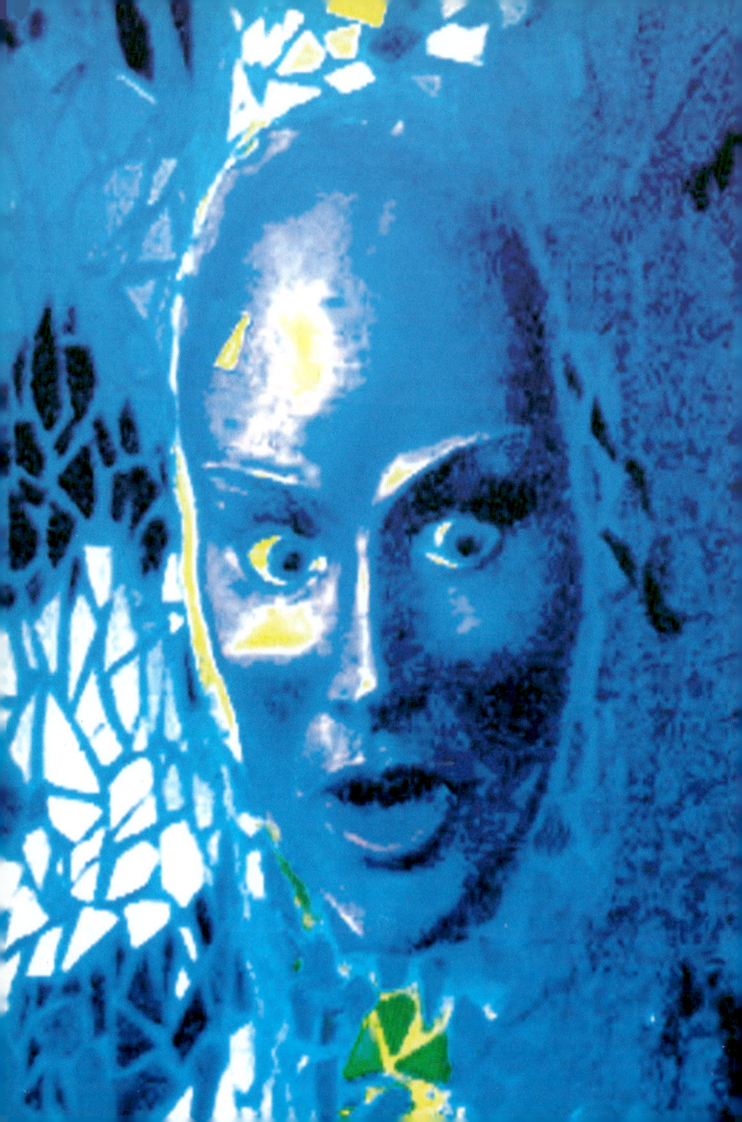

# Turk's Head
## Parliament Street

**19**

At the end of the rollercoaster ride called *evening time in bars central*, after stepping over bodies and predictable guitars, The Turk's Head remains a popular destination, sparkling fantastically blue and orange (sometimes aquamarine) in Moroccan mosaic, forming the shape of Dublin's most *unusual* looking bar. Figures and faces burst out of the columns, dancing 30's icons echoing Harlow, vaguely Dietrich, enlivening an otherwise empty shell. There are some great murals out the back which I found myself transfixed by one Friday night as the *Euro-pickup, kebab and throw-up* crowd caned it maniacally about me. Such is the curse of being at the end of Temple Bar. Well, that's the excuse I have chosen..

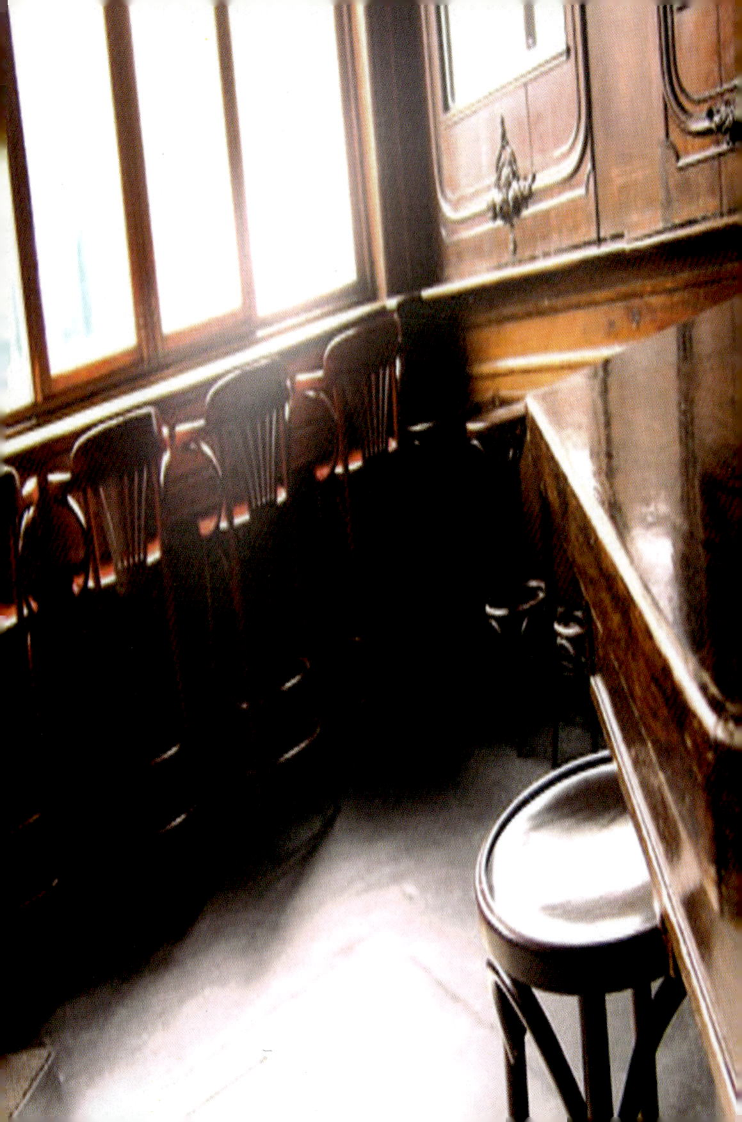

# The Oak
## Dame Street

**20**

The Oak is an unusual vaudevillian spot, and if you've just stepped out of the theatre then coming here is like stepping into another. With its dark sweeping curtains and authentic attention to detail you could imagine this being a luvvies paradise, but it's not. In fact, while in here, a luvvie of sorts approached the counter (probably for the first time in her life) crying out dramatically (and this *is* how it happened), *I say! What do you offer in the way of snacks?* To which the roguish wit behind the ramp, to yer wan's chagrin, replied, *Guinness......or crisps*. Which in my opinion deserved a standing ovation but was settled on wry grins all round. I do like The Oak but it really does remind me of an old wooden bar in Amsterdam which I just can't get out of my head whenever I'm in here. Of course, Dublin's Oak has far higher moral standards but with a couple of gins and a whim of imagination, it wouldn't be hard to imagine a turn of the century boudoir behind one of those drapes.

BROGAN'S BAR 75

# Brogan's
## Dame Street

**21**

If the measure of perfect hospitality is in the homeliness of the welcome, then this pub is like stepping into your Auntie's cottage kitchen. You really feel like you're in someone's private room and this, (pleasantly), demands a mutual level of respect from punter and landlord alike. I mean, what better place to stay and spend money, than one in which you are totally relaxed. (Pub designers take heed!) I was all for taking off my shoes and socks and resting my tired plates up on a stool, pint in one hand, remote control in the other. With the household telly hitched up on a crate surrounded by teacups and general personal flotsam, you'd hardly believe this was a city centre bar – more the wilds of Leitrim or some such quieter environment. Come here pre or post Olympia or simply for fond hearthsidelike warmth and amiability.

# Irish Film Institute
## Eustace Street

**22**

You know, it's always a treat when you discover a place you've never been to before, that you like immediately, for reasons unbeknown other than that you think it's your little secret to pass on at your discretion to those who you feel deserve it. All acceptable reasons, I admit, for contacting a psychiatrist but, in this case, the power-crazy selfish motive can be allowed – even if just to prove that civilization does exist in Temple Bar on a weekend night. I was actually going to leave out this bar just because I like it as it is. Tall, refined, hidden. It's one of the places you either know or you don't. A bit like films, in my experience. And a bit like some of the conversations you're likely to hear in here. Some know, some don't. Some pretend to know, some pretend to *not* know. Some couldn't care less and just want an hour in the corner booth. I think I've said too much.

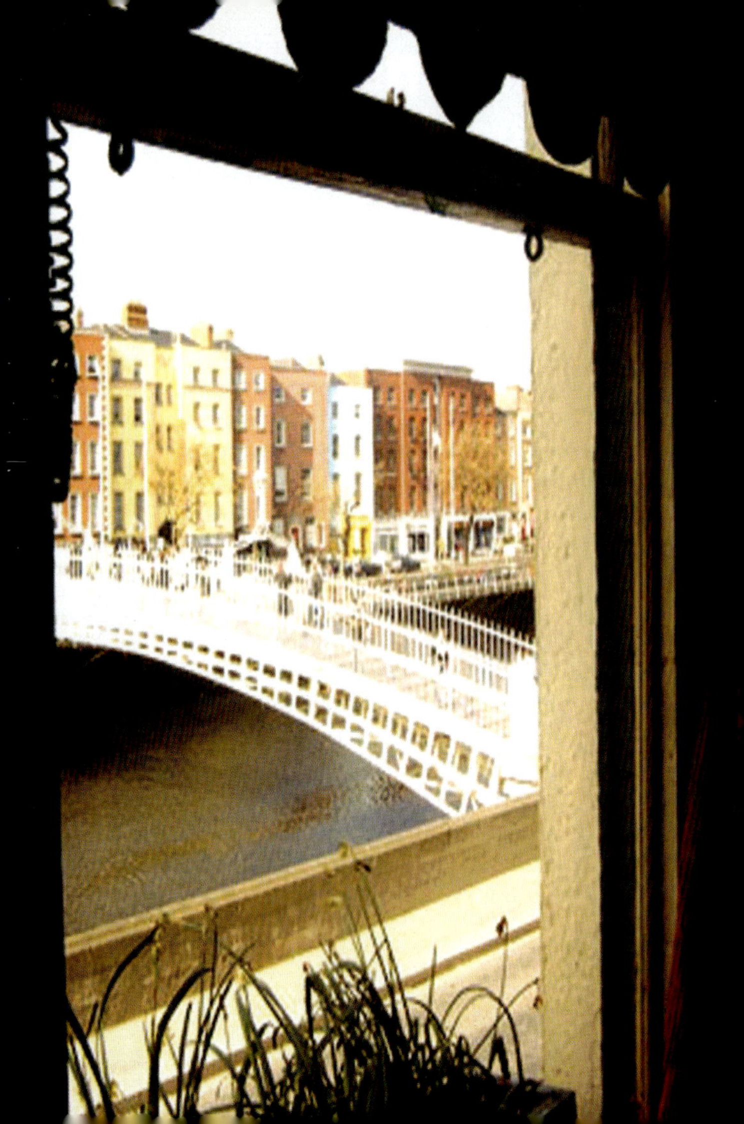

# Ha'penny Bridge Inn
## Wellington Quay

**23**

Ha'penny! Ha'penny! Come to me, Ha'penny! This is one of my favourite pubs in the world – so *shhh* – don't tell everybody. Within earshot of the filthy beer octopuses of Temple Bar, yet a million miles away intellectually, this place is truly a haven. Escaping the cutting Dublin winter wind, nipping into here can have you feel like a weary sailor returned to home port. (If you're looking for weary sailors, by the way, try elsewhere. It was merely an illustration emphasizing the Welcome v Thirst Satisfaction ratio.) Another no-nonsense affair whose characterful décor merely adds to brighten the varied gathered conversationalists. I pray it doesn't change. The Ha'penny's entertainment is absolutely unsurpassable. *How's that for a soundbite?* – well it's true and once you've had a taste, you'll be hooked. By the way, one of the best Liffey views is to be had from the upstairs bar.

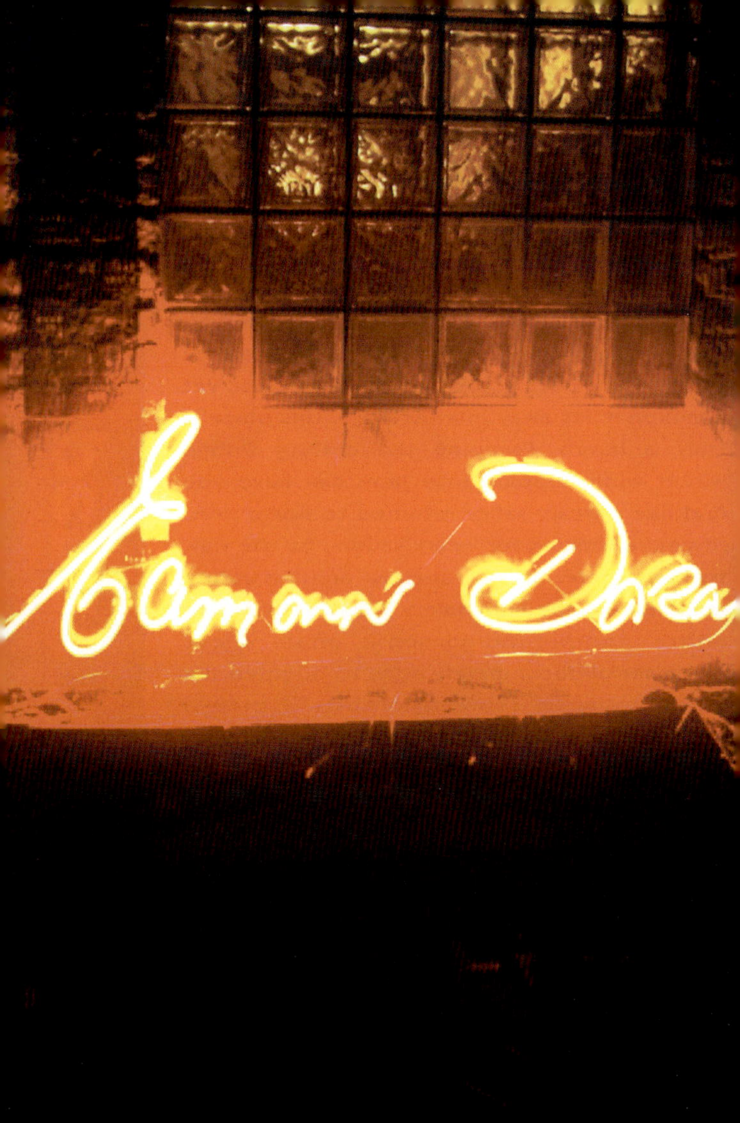

# Eamon Doran's
## Crown Alley

**24**

I stumbled into this place early once, (after being up all night at a soup-tasting contest, I craved the comfort of darkness), to revive my aching soul and tired head with the food of champions. As I slipped down the last steps, there was a young group playing their little hearts out – *The sun was coming up / I took a stroll / I think I may have lost control / That's what you get for drinkin' in this hole* - singing the tune to my day and endearing themselves to me immediately and all of the other gathered drunkulars. Art v life etc. Anyway, the point is, Eamon's is a feeding ground for the up-and-coming and music abounds almost all day, every day (or so it seems everytime I've been in). And when there are no bands on there is a cracking jukebox. The soul of the Dublin music scene resides somewhere in this basement dungeon and is alive and well! I promise you. Instinctively, this is a great place to hide.

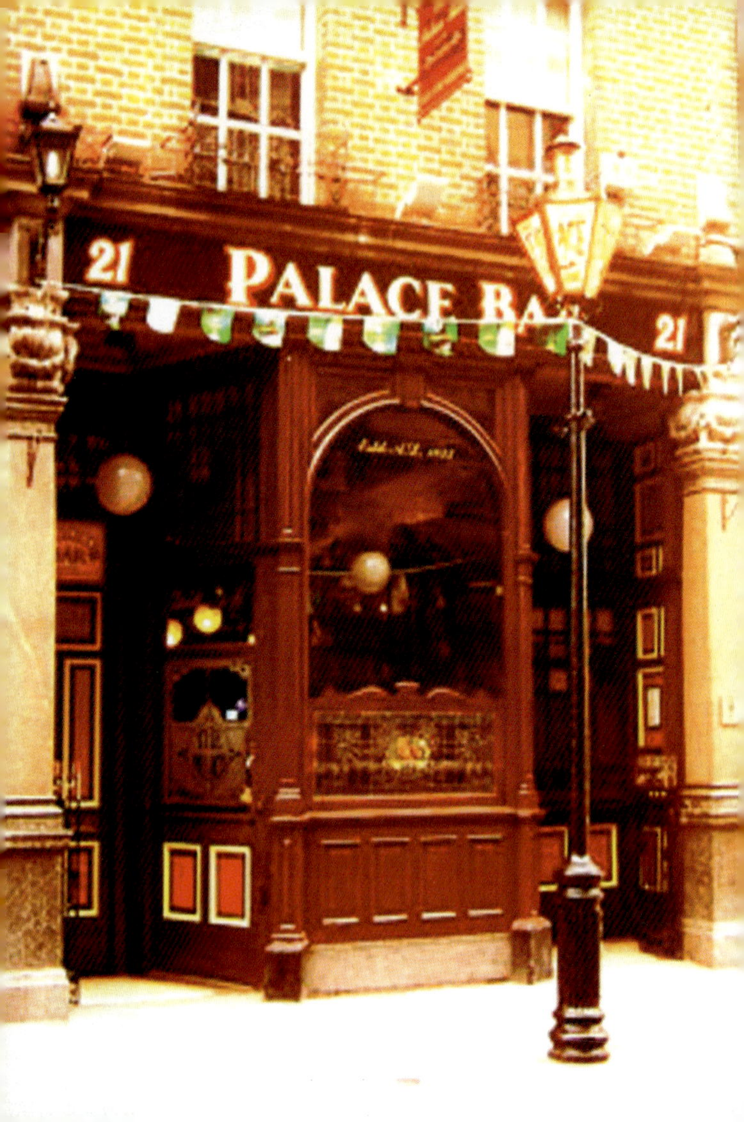
21
PALACE BA
21

# Palace Bar
## Fleet Street

**25**

Steeped in literary legend, The Palace has hosted more articulate behemoths than any university you might care to mention, taking unreservedly their inspiration from the very soul of a bar whose constant flow of words was energetic and intoxicating. With so many ideas bouncing back and forth off the walls and partitions, then surely the very atoms of this place must be completely intertwined with the lost gems of geniuses long gone, thought up and, just as quickly, forgotten in the mindswirl of a creamy stout. Grabbing just a piece of that is what, to me, The Palace oozes perfectly and magnetically. To others, it is the well-respected old relative that absolutely *everybody* knows and remembers fondly, whose charms need no introduction to many, many Dubliners - and particularly those who appreciate a proper pint. The bar is cordial and social, the lounge, contemplative and a great haven in the still mid-afternoon.

Palace Bar

BOWES

GUINN

# Bowe's
## Fleet Street

**26**

*Meet me under Bowe's clock* as remembered in the famous street ditty, (had it ever been written). The point is, it could have been, because Bowe's clock is South City's answer to Clery's and as familiar a sight to hacks, printers and busmen as it was fifty years ago. Completely unpretentious, this is a Dublin pub with its heart on its sleeve. A no-nonsense pub's pub. The way they're supposed to be. I would come here purely because of that - and so should you. If the barman doesn't tell you a joke, don't be offended. These are pros, remember, and it's a serious business. Talking of jokes, I could tell you an embarrassing story about Singles Night here about seven years ago – but I won't. Go get your own.

Bowe's

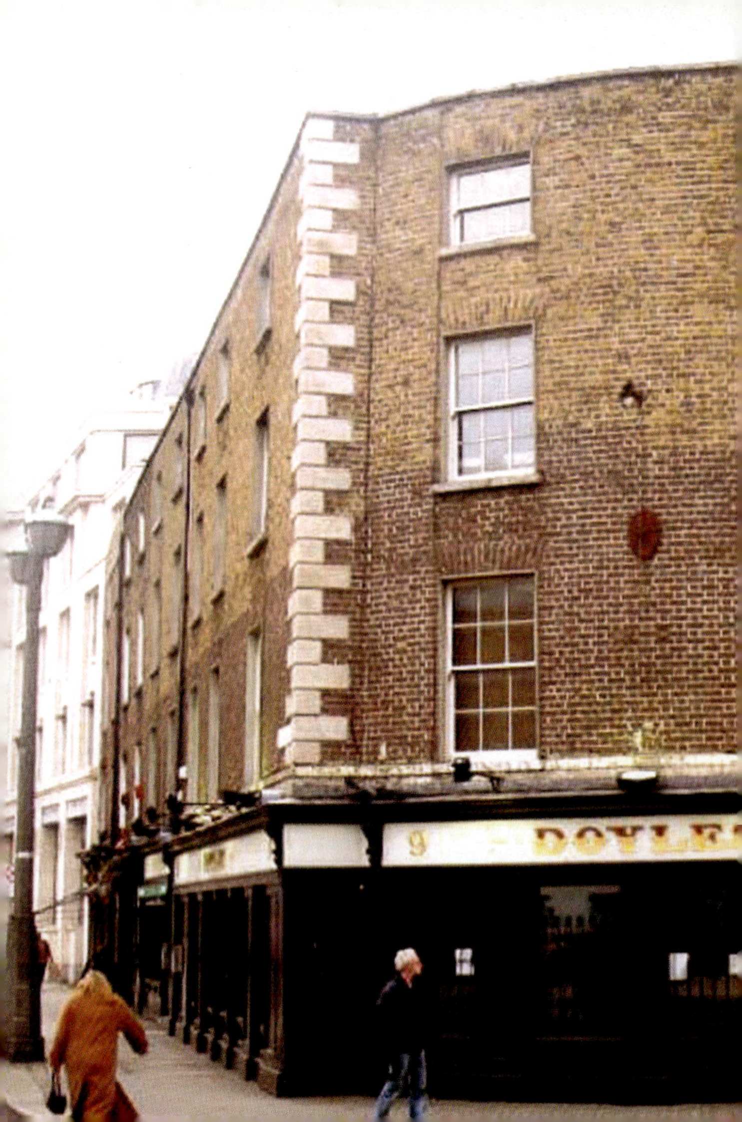
9
DOYLE

# Doyle's
## College Street

**27**

As familiar a sight to Trinity students as the Parliament Square campanile, Doyle's might as well be marked on their timetables as a necessary part of the course. I've heard of seminars being held in here by thirst-challenged professors (aren't they all?) but that's not a regular slot, so no need to give up the day-job yet in the hope of a free (but drunken) education. This is certainly not the kind of place to go to contemplate the complexities of individuality and universality because you won't be able to. There is *always* something going on. It is constantly moving. *Philosophy in itself, methinks...* In addition to the blurring parade, Doyle's is another venue gaining respect for top quality hosting of musical nights and the acoustic evenings are sound affairs.

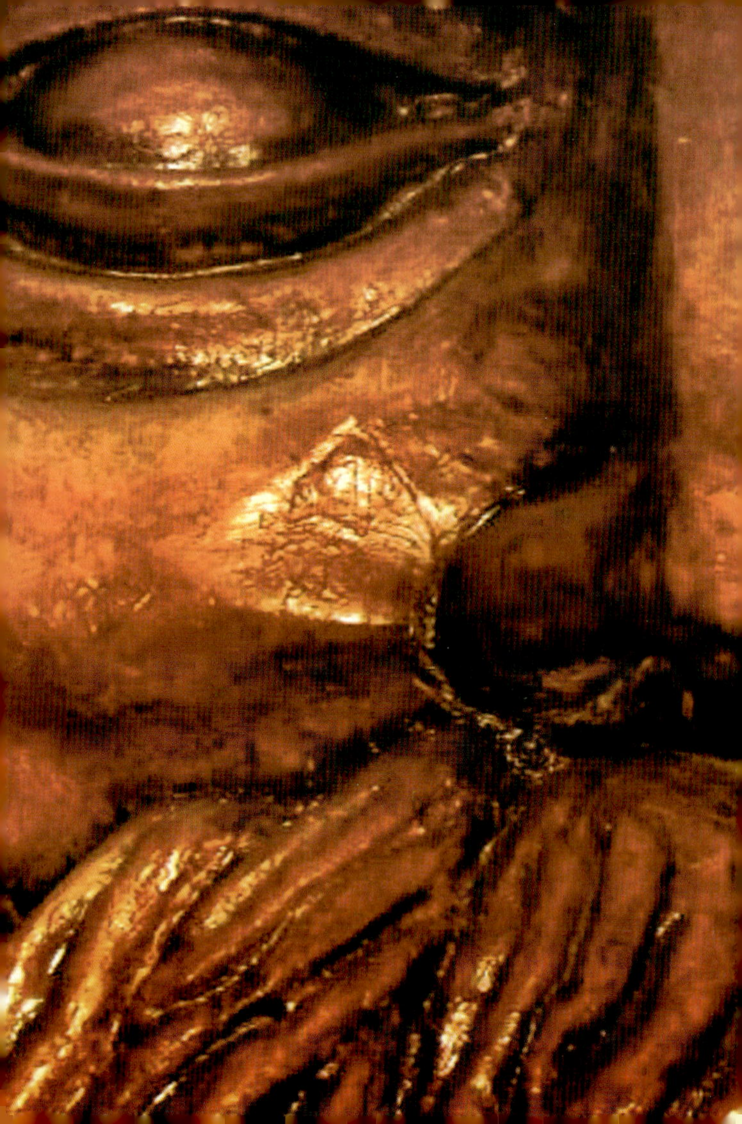

# Long Stone
## Townsend Street

**28**

A monstrous fiery gargoyle insists on your warm welcome in this unusual, but interesting, mishmash of pub, museum and mediaeval hall. Actually, it's a representation of the Viking warmth god, a spectacular and symbolic nod to the origins of this ancient city and always a focus of conversation or wistful daydreaming. Low-lighting, fading friezes, dark wood and high ceiling all combine to instil a cathedral-like environment which is then utterly belied by the far from solemn atmosphere that makes for a genuinely lively congregation come the weekend or, indeed, lunchtime. It is a quirky pub, simply because you cannot pigeon-hole it or its clientele. Close to Trinity, buses, the cinema, the Dart, even the Garda station, you are guaranteed only one thing – a multifarious cocktail – and surely that's the sign (and purpose) of a great pub.

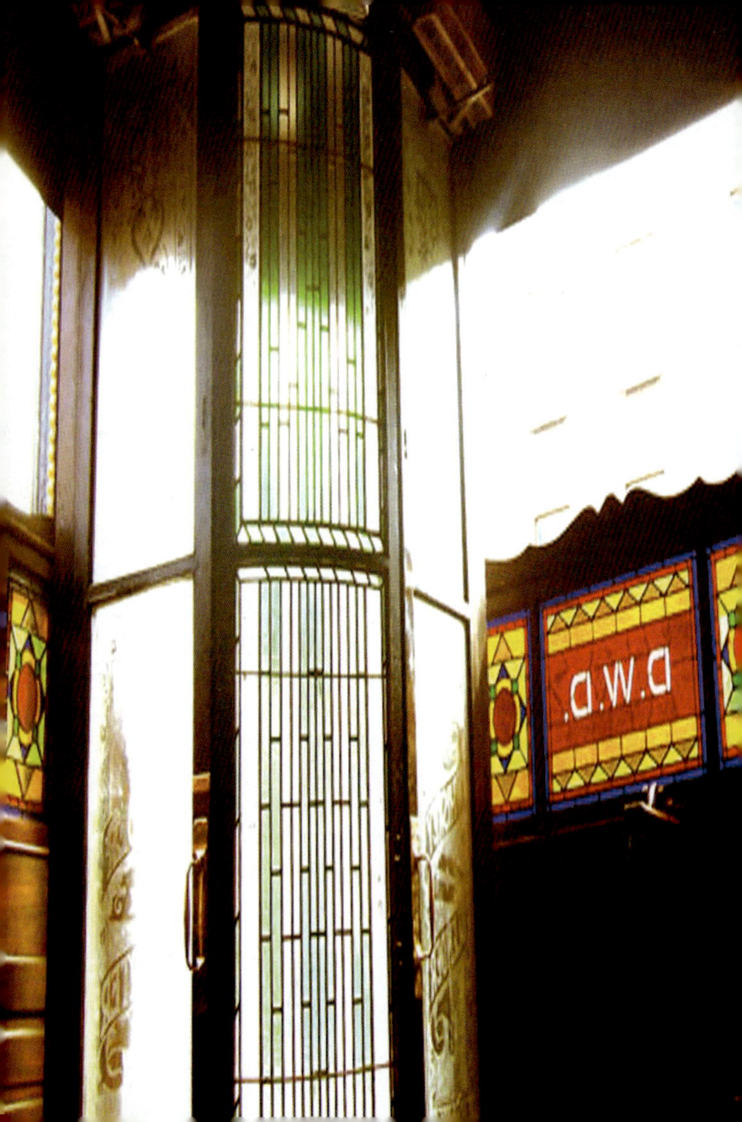

# O'Neill's
## Pearse Street

**29**

I was sat in here one afternoon, watching the rays passing through the stained-glass window raisers and pondered on why so many other pubs have removed them. Okay, they might argue that they want to show the inside to the outside and encourage punters to enter but they fail to see their underlying purpose. That is, to keep the punter *inside*. Enthralled in his/her own private world without having to care for one second about what the outside world (that being beyond the perimeters of the house) is thinking, let alone doing. This is where old wins, hands-down, over new and O'Neill's, in that, is a comforting revelation. The bar here is just made for philosophising - circular, complete and quietly in motion (no I hadn't had ten pints, it's allegorical) and the corner door! Well, I promise you. It is like a portal out of some maelstrom, and escaping the manic traffic of Pearse Street into this house, you will see what I mean.

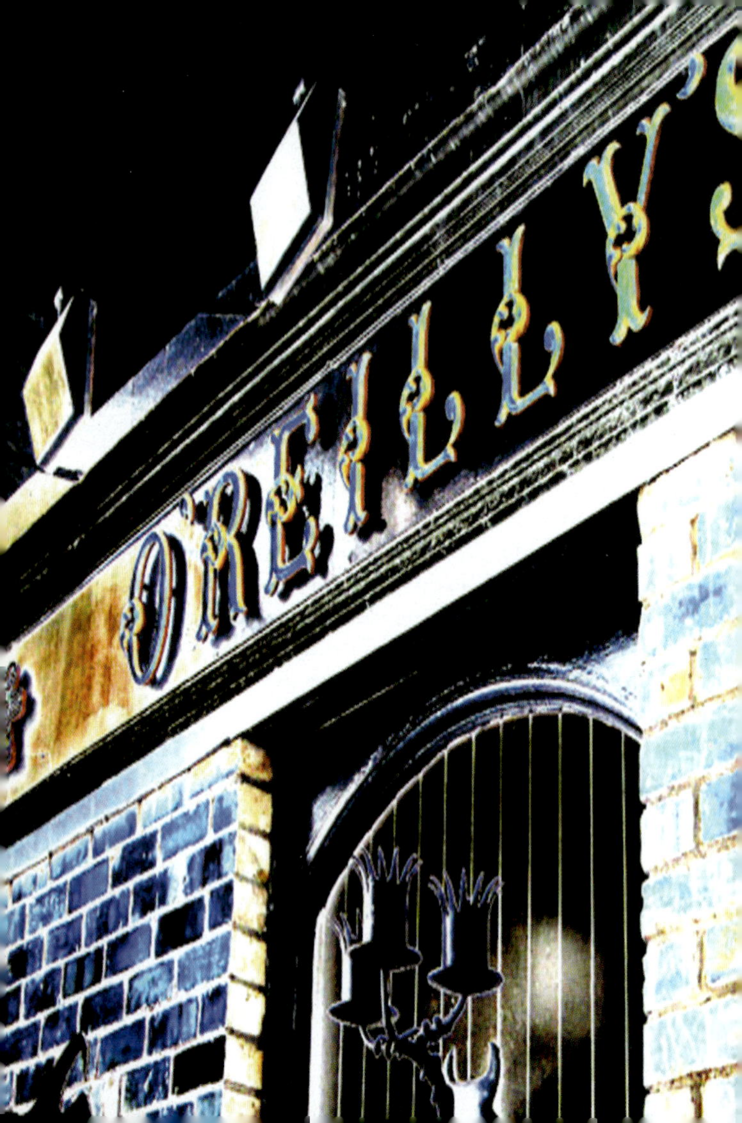
O'REILLY'S

# O'Reilly's
## Luke Street

**30**

Two totally different people, of different ages suggested I include this in the book. One would regularly pop in on the way home via Tara Street and the other was in for a night with friends. Both, however, had the identically accurate description: *Weird*. And that's not *weird* in a negative sense, more simply, *mad*. Basically, it's not what you would expect, bang in the middle of the city, but that's what makes it refreshing. You can have too many mirrors and brass pumps and something *out there* adds nicely to the mix. Even though you may think you've entered either a torture chamber or a dominatrix's lair, you'll soon settle into the chilled-out (if mediaeval) tones of this ground floor cellar. Banquet tables and candlelight, flaming lamps and DJ's pulpit - all under the gaze of the classical Custom House. Hard to imagine? Well, yeah - but so what?

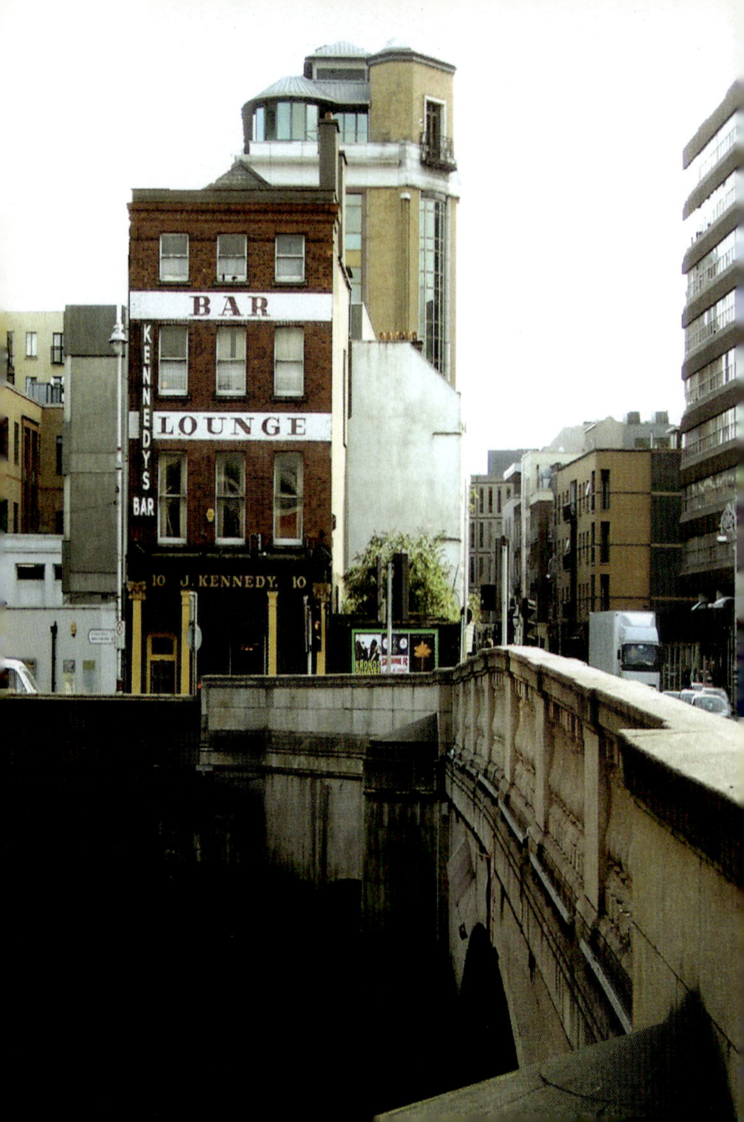
BAR
KENNEDYS BAR
LOUNGE
10 J. KENNEDY. 10

# Kennedy's
## George's Quay

**31**

Yeh! That one by Butt Bridge with the blinds and the neons. Yes! The one next to Tara Street Dart. No! Not the other one. With two famous Kennedy's in Dublin (relatively close) it might be easy to mix them up but once you *know* this one, you won't forget it. I mean, this is a Liffey landmark. Think of all the hoardes of travellers and tourists who've come off buses and ships and walked in toward the city centre. They will all have seen Kennedy's and thought, *Yes. I would like a pint in there.* And whether they did or not is by the by, the point is, they were correct. If JFK had visited here when he was on the lash in Dublin (he famously went to Mulligan's), he could well have seen the same decor that you will see today. Very sixties, a little kitch, but absolutely sincere. It is a personable and relaxing place and it's one of those houses that I pray does not change. I truly felt a bohemian vibration about this place and, no, it wasn't a train passing over. In Dublin, you tend to get the very new or the very old. Well, here's nicely inbetween, with the kind of affable host that used to set aside Dublin's pubs as, without doubt, the most unique and enjoyable on the planet.

EST. 1782

# Mulligan's
## Poolbeg Street

**32**

Friend of presidents and paupers, John Mulligan's doorway is probably the most famous pub façade known to humankind. You could be in downtown Accra and I guarantee if there is an Irish theme bar, there will somewhere be a picture of Mulligan's. In fact, to avoid the tourist trap implied by over-exposure, I used to avoid this shop but hold my hands up now and beg John for forgiveness – for I have seen the error of my ways after meeting some friends in here and immediately was charmed. A veritable tardis of a place, you could easily lose yourself somewhere in this fertile hotbed of character and conviviality – and I think that is a fine idea. A great pint, in great surroundings with a regularly good-humoured crowd. Summer in the city. Yahoo!

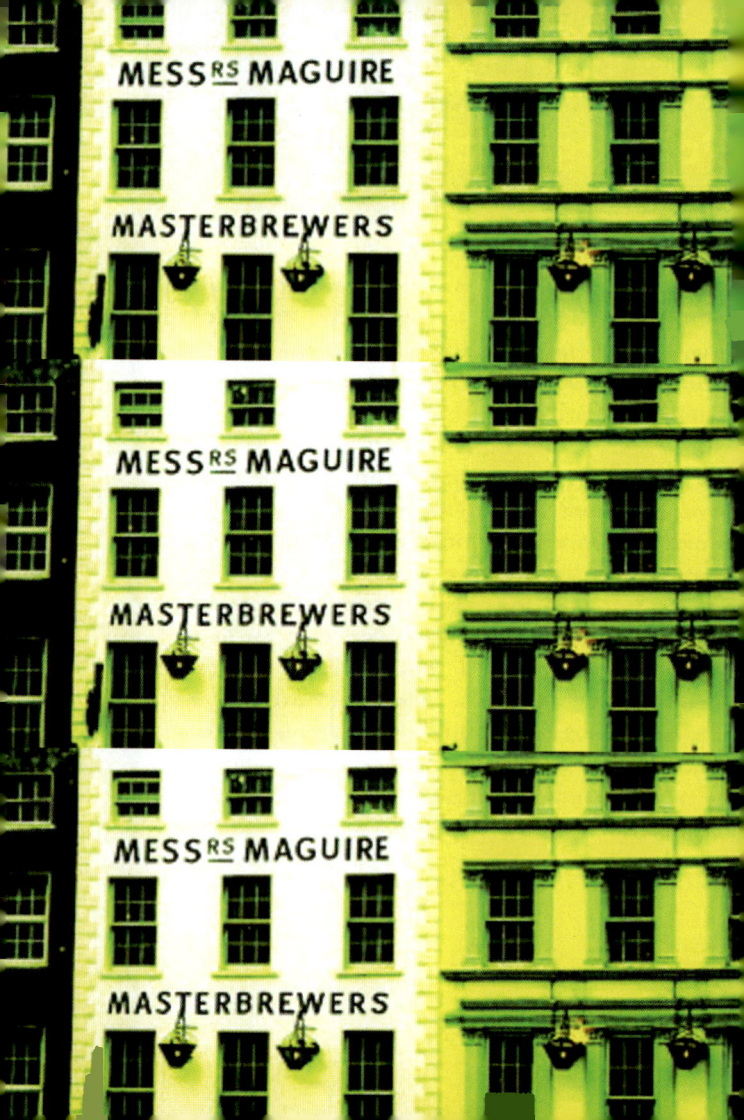

MESS RS MAGUIRE

MASTERBREWERS

MESS RS MAGUIRE

MASTERBREWERS

MESS RS MAGUIRE

MASTERBREWERS

# Messrs. Maguire
## Burgh Quay

**33**

There are some naysayers in this town who would rather not enjoy the spectacular view of a revamped O'Connell Street, bridge, G.P.O., spire and Liffey in comfortable surroundings with a nice pint. They would rather sit at home or in the office looking at the scene via a stilted webcam, all safe and stiff. Well I say *NAY* to all that nonsense, a fine vista is a fine vista and I have brought visitors to Dublin up here to combine such prospects with raucous consumption. An ideal world, is it not? Save tramping around in dayglo shorts, crowd-weaving and developing new and unknown animosities to fellow man. Am I not a great help altogether? Additionally, Messrs. has plenty of room, multitudinous hideaways and ranges from contemplative and calm to blisteringly mental, depending, of course, on your chosen time of potation.

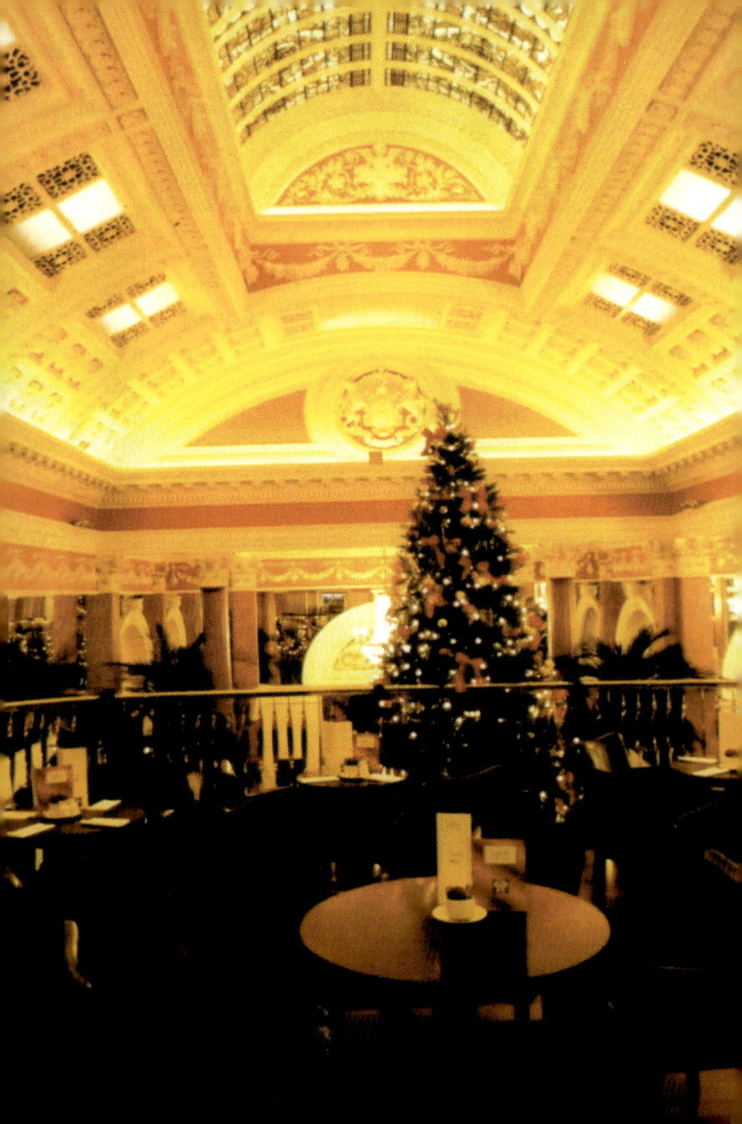

# The Bank
## College Green

**34**

Wouldn't it be an ideal world we lived in, if banks served alcohol. That loan refusal really wouldn't be such a blow if cushioned by a complimentary double scotch...Oh well – back to the real world – this spectacularly airy (bring a scarf) building has been kept so close to the original bank design that all that is missing is nonchalant tellers and never-ending queues. Nevertheless, in their place you get a great choice in the beverage deposit option, prime foodstuffs and one of the most beautiful interiors this fair city has to offer. (Don't fall off your stool as you gaze on the stained-glass heavens.) And on your way out, don't say goodnight to the seven foot bouncer (like I did), he's a statue – or just plain ignorant. Let's put it this way, he's the quiet type.

# FOGGY DEW

Nº I.   Nº I.

# Foggy Dew
## Fownes Street Upper

35

I like reproduction, don't get me wrong. But not so much *in* or *of* public houses. But then I would much rather see a faithful reconstruction of a turn of the century (*that'll be the one before last*) Dublin house, than be subjected to an icy chrome and pine furniture showroom that happens to serve alcohol – in silly glasses. So it's full marks to the Dew for retaining a traditional style and tipping its hat in recognition to Dublin's proud history and protagonists (*great moody portraits by the way*) shamed daily by the rivers of vomit that regularly flood this particular area. This pub is basically a safe bet with a decent mixed crowd but can get a little crowded come Saturday night. But then again, show me somewhere that doesn't. Central Dublin at 3am is probably busier than a normal lunchtime because the world and his sister, dog, extended family and home contents are out on the sauce in a fine, fearless fashion. N.B. The Dew has good live music on Sunday evenings.

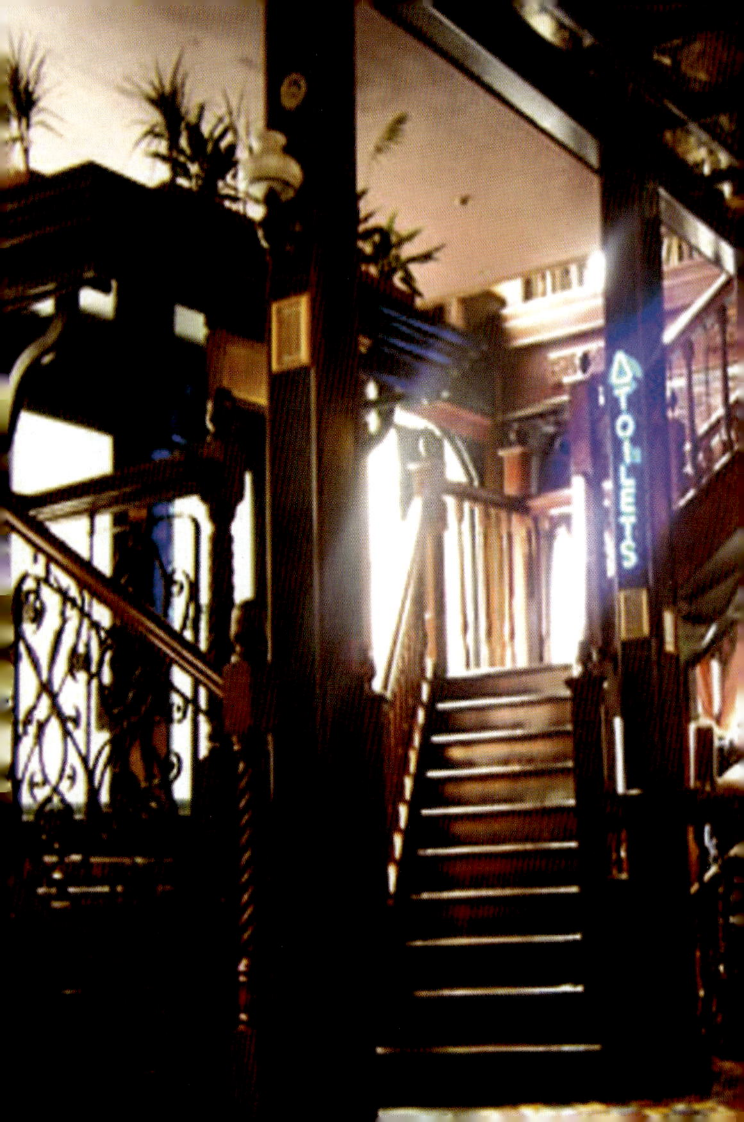
TOILETS

# Trinity Arch
## Dame Street

**36**

Trinity Arch is a favourite of several Trinity students I know, even though it's not your usual dank or nasty student type haunt. In fact, the Arch is quite refined, a reasonably sane place to escape to from the flurry of populace a la Dame Street. Sit up on the raised platform between floors, and gaze over the rush-hour flanked by palms and the kind of implied luxury that puts you in the mind of some lofty old Raj hill station – just replace the tea with stout and you're there! One of the things that always makes an impression on me is how many people actually *know* a particular bar. And if they report it favourably then there is definitely something right going on. (Unless of course, they're all on the payroll, and even in the most advanced state of cynicism, that is unlikely). So, surely there is all the recommendation you need. As a nightspot, Trinity Arch is a jumping, entertaining mix – one of the best in the city centre. All you require for a night here is a good sense of direction to return you safely from the great toilet traverse. You'll see what I mean.

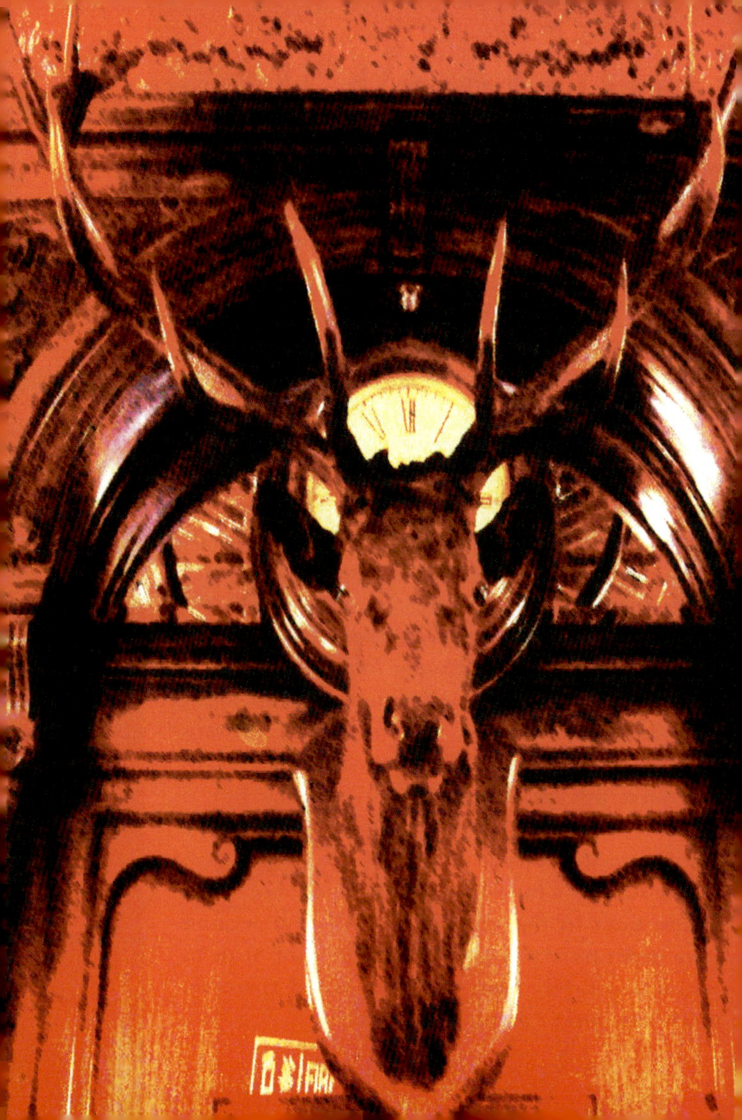

# Stag's Head
## Dame Court

**37**

An old friend of mine used to have a phobia about old mirrors – the more antique, the more phobic. She was uneased by imagining all the ancient faces that had looked from *this* side into the very same glass, and were now potentially staring out from the other. She may well have been drunk or even insightful because every time I come in here, I look in the huge back-bar mirrors and think on all the faces, brilliant and otherwise, that have adorned this grand old lady and how impressed they must be by the absolute lack of renovation that clinks nightly and mystically right back to 1895. The front bar always reminds me of a great railway station bar, constantly moving, re-energizing itself, absolutely functional. Whereas the back lounge is a deep, dark wonder of plush calm, where retreat into which brings forth a contemplative and reflective glow. A collegiate associate informed me that Joyce used to drink here. Well, if it's good enough for the greatest writer of the twentieth century etc..etc...

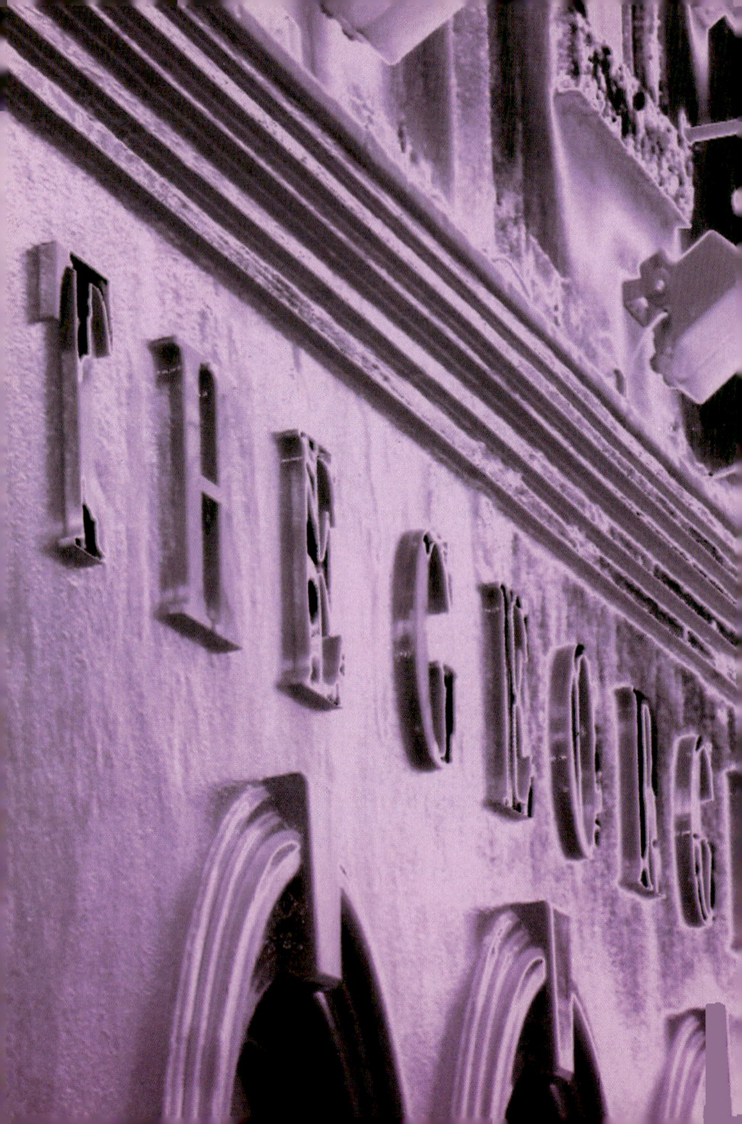

# The George
## Sth. Great George's St.

**38**

The George stands proudly in its infamy promising *Bona Palare* and all those other gay-bar clichés, that might have been true in 1950's Soho and, if the truth be told, unfairly categorize places like this in the eyes of those who have never or *would never* come here for whatever reason. Even the smoked glass frontage only adds to the mythology belying the fact that inside is far from secluded, dark and deviant but one of Dublin's *goodtime* bars. And that means a good time for whoever you are or whatever your orientation. The front bar, all purples and pinks is the nightclubby modern scene whereas out back, the more traditional bar. All you've got to do is lighten up and live it up! Because this is where it happens. It'd be nice to see that darkened glass go - Ireland, (particularly its youth), is a lot more liberal (and European) than you might think.

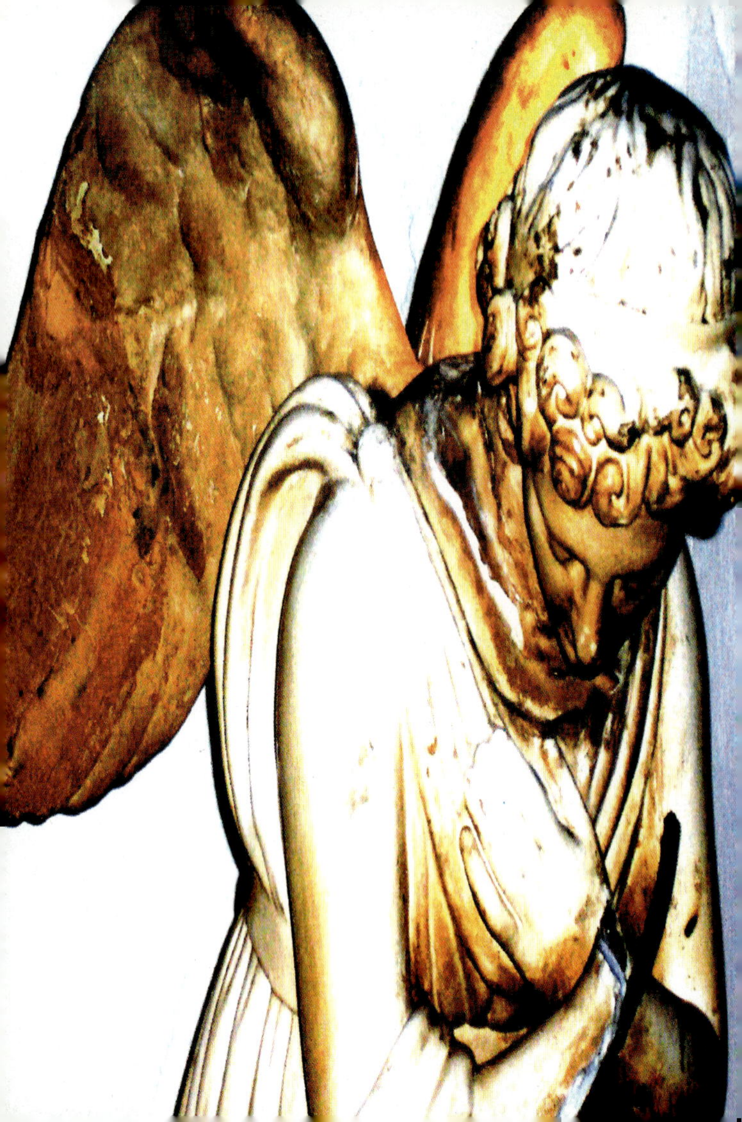

# The Globe
## Sth. Great George's St.

**39**

The only word I could summon up to *really* paint the portrait of The Globe and grab it wholeheartedly, is *SEXY*. Yes and all the mystery therein! I agree, it's not a word often used to associate with drinking in Dublin, but so what? Let's start here. With a definite Greenwich Village vibe, that means a varied fairly bohemian atmosphere with a little pretension (you must learn to expect this) but not enough to be over-bearing or flatulent. One of the most enduring images I ever witnessed was in here one smoky afternoon many lovely years ago - an image that Bord Failte or Guinness would love to adopt. That is of wholesome Irish loveliness combined with indulgent, intentional sin. This freckled and dark vision of wild beauty taking up her foaming pint pot and imbibing as a shore receives the tide before wiping the residue with the back of her hand. There is a heaven. I've seen it.

The Globe

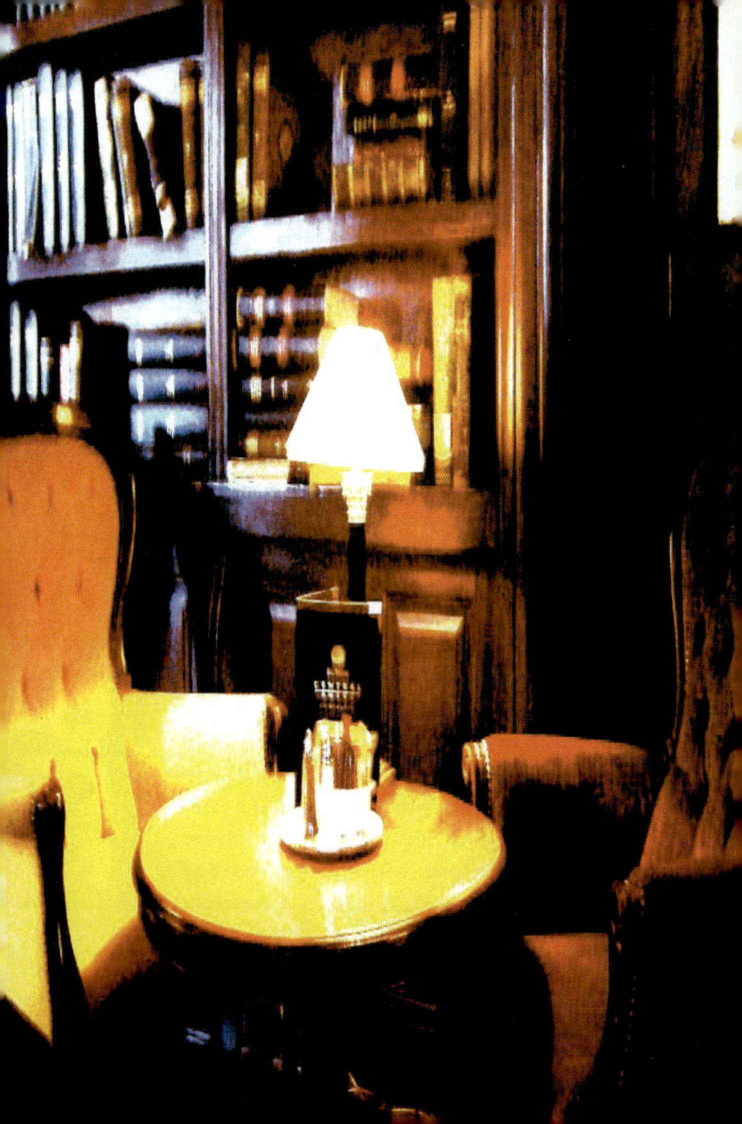

# Library Bar
## Exchequer Street

**40**

Conducive wholly to both animated musing and furrowed philosophy, here, the greatest library in town. Oozing grandeur and individual class, there is an enviable perpetual decorum maintained which *just makes such a nice change!* Is it the floor-to-ceiling books? The drawing-room décor? The luxurious furnishings? The elevated position? Somehow it's all of these and their combination with several placid pints can very easily lead to a state of tranquility. Sitting by the open window on a summer evening, you feel like you're ten floors up over Broadway; the voices, the shouting, the sirens, the whole melée a mile or more below you - utterly beyond concern or even contempt. Such is the cocoon-like magic of this particular establishment. Traditionally, you would probably regard The Library Bar as un-Dublin as can be - more akin to some ghastly exclusive brandy and cigars choke club on Regent Street - but you'd be surprised. The Dublin clientelle is as varied as the modern metropolis and selfishly, delightfully discerning when it comes to places like this.

Library Bar

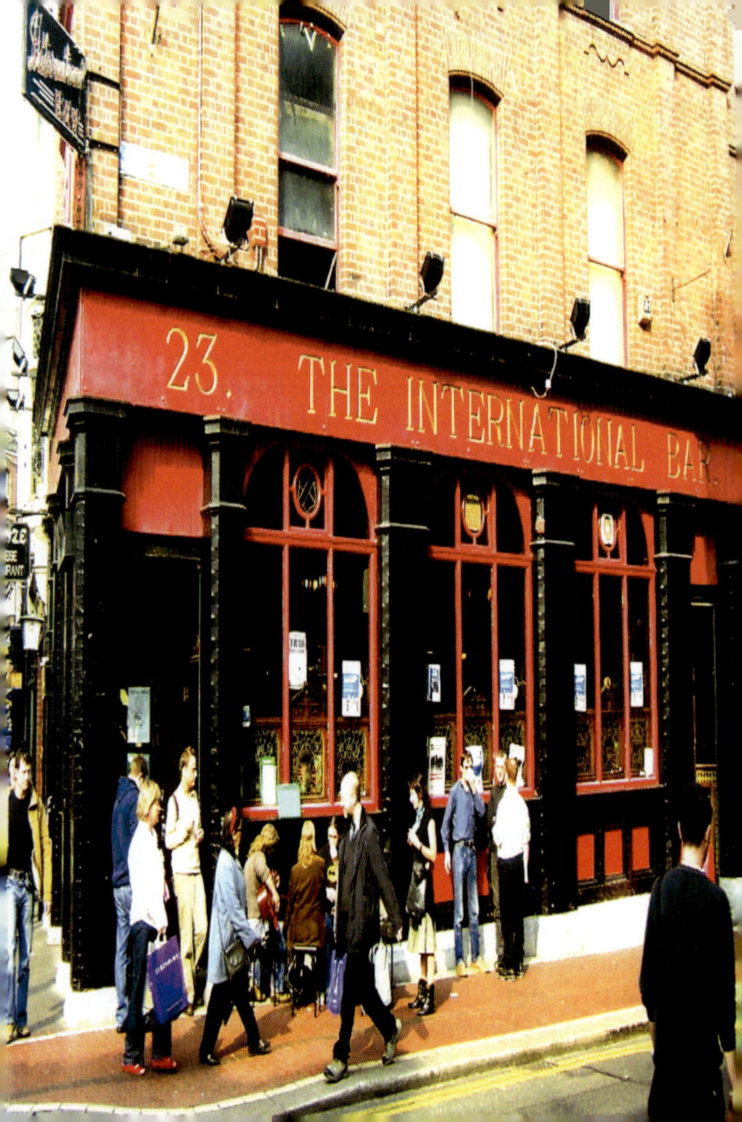
23. THE INTERNATIONAL BAR.

# The International
## Wicklow Street

**41**

The dour and solemn corner edifice that signifies the location of The International, is a decidedly misleading indication in terms of the comedic profusion that has blossomed here in the last fifteen years. In fact, the varying music nights are similarly respected and well-attended - most of them held in the upstairs Cellar. (If that confuses you or you don't *get it* then maybe you ought to give stand-up a miss. It may upset you.) Of course, extra-curricular activities are not to every punter's taste and, as a free alternative, a handful of pints in the saloon bar should be sufficient entertainment even for the stoniest hearts. I mean, just stare at the characters carved in the bar! They stand as if the building was built around their ancient knowledge. Look through mirror to antique mirror - you'll see the Answer. *WHISKEY POWERS.....*

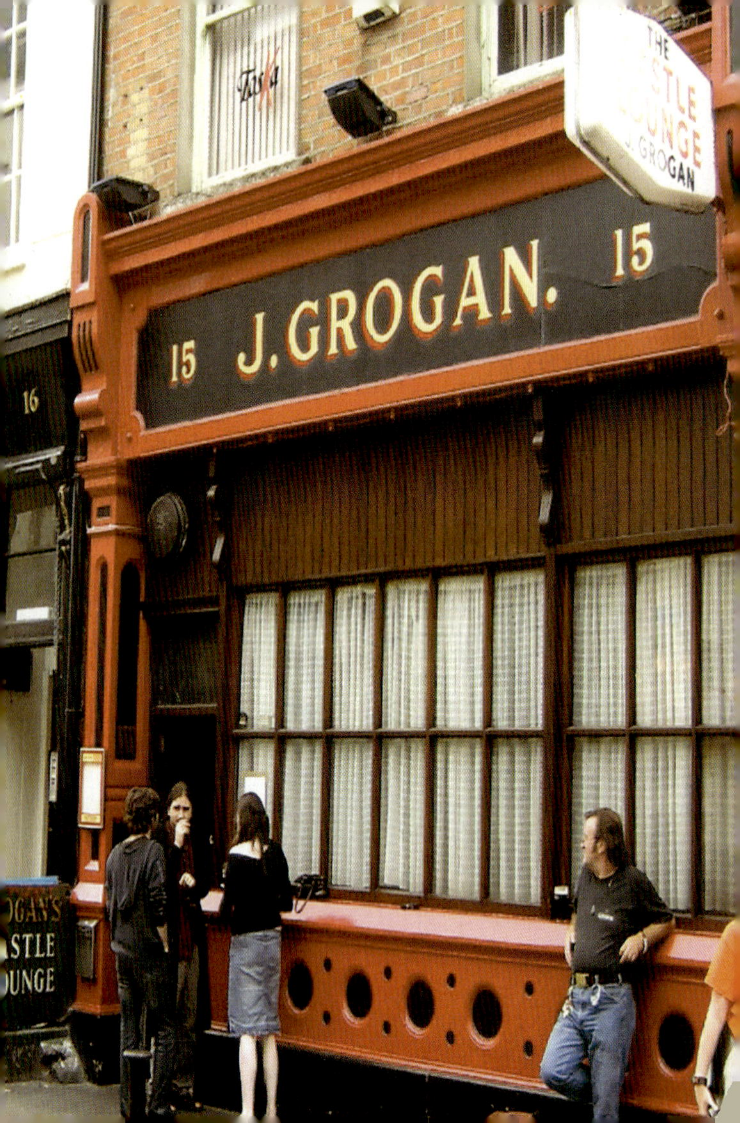
15
J. GROGAN.
15
J. GROGAN
16

# Grogan's
## South William Street

**42**

The very first time I came to this place, I thought I'd stepped aboard the Marie Celeste – there was not a soul on board (okay it was early) but it gave me the perfect and lasting first impression (of tranquillity and finely-furrowed peaceful pondering) which I always return to when I think on this place. If Messrs. Behan, O'Nolan, Kavanagh, O'Casey et al were now spiritually housed in some ethereal literary shebeen eternal, then I imagine it would look a lot like this. In fact, with the softly diffused daylight, stained-glass decoration and the kind of soft carpet that kindly silences the footsteps of sinners, this could have been the inspiration for many "new" church designs. With endlessly engaging host and wistful daydream inducing surroundings, the home of the poets and philosophers is in safe hands. Think on, drink on, stay here forever.

Grogan's

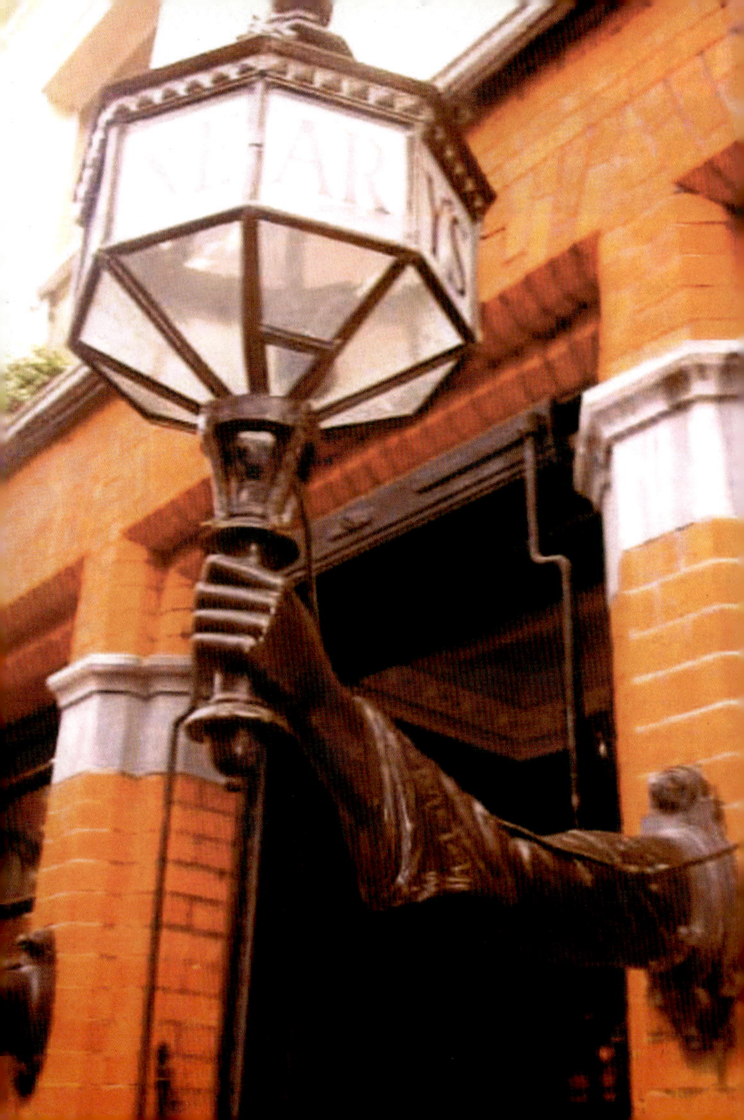

# Neary's
## Chatham Street

**43**

Red and immaculate like the veritable cardinal's boudoir (one might imagine..) is the lasting and definitive image I have of Nearey's. Like a four-star hotel lobby bar transported directly from 1930, this place deserves respect and, tastefully, demands it, encouraging refinement and finesse from its varied patrons – leading, if you like, by classic example. You will never see rowdy beer monstering within these walls and that is a truly blessed relief for the kind of humble soul who just wants a peaceful and relaxing drink. Come evening time, a more theatrical air descends, *Dahhling*, and rubbing shoulders with star of stage or, indeed, backstage can well be de rigeur, clinking politely, maintaining restraint in guffaw, all under the gaslamp gaze of Edwardian splendour.

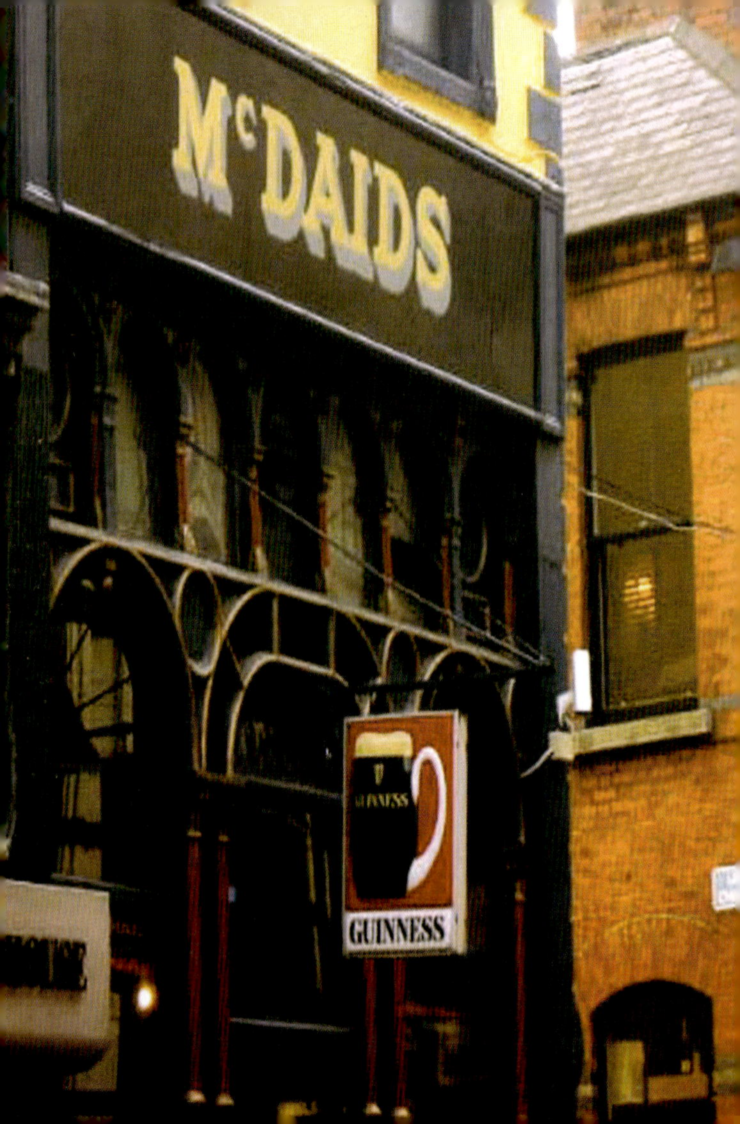
McDAIDS
GUINNESS
GUINNESS

# McDaid's
## Harry Street

**44**

Dublin's most famous ex-morgue has certainly seen a few pickled onions, one would expect, considering the multi-million tourist trade in literary legends that adorns every tea-towel, postcard and pack of biccies, all proclaiming *HERE!* to be the centre of the universe. And well it might have been between 1930 and 1960 and LONG MAY WE NOT FORGET IT (OR THEM) - but trying to reheat a soufflé, as Paul McCartney once quipped, is impossible and raises just a touch of cynical sneer from the average Dubliner who values McDaid's as part of the old school and somewhere to get a good pint without having to stumble over naively ambitious pseudo- geniuses and their reams of hastily scribbled manuscripts hoping to be discovered, or uncovered, for that matter. But there you go! I guess that's what happens when your reputation goes before you.

**McDaid's**

BRUXELLES

# Bruxelles

## Harry Street

**45**

Could you possibly conceive the mean and sweaty crew of Iron Maiden or some other such fearsome musical combo, gently sipping espressos on the Champs-Elysées? No? Neither could I, but here, where rock meets refined, it would certainly not be an alien concept. Bruxelles, the indie kids hideout and bikers' lair, has metamorphosed nicely, albeit gradually and continuously, into as perfect a European model of pavement drinking that Ireland could possibly muster without crossing the fine line of inanity and self-obsession. Consequently, it is the envy, on a sunny afternoon, of every pub/café without an outdoor area. Downstairs is still the unpredictable, heavy-rock crypt that it always has been but if you ask any self-respecting member of the human race to choose between an evening of spandex and death or bang bang predictable monotones then I suspect you will find them edging in this direction.

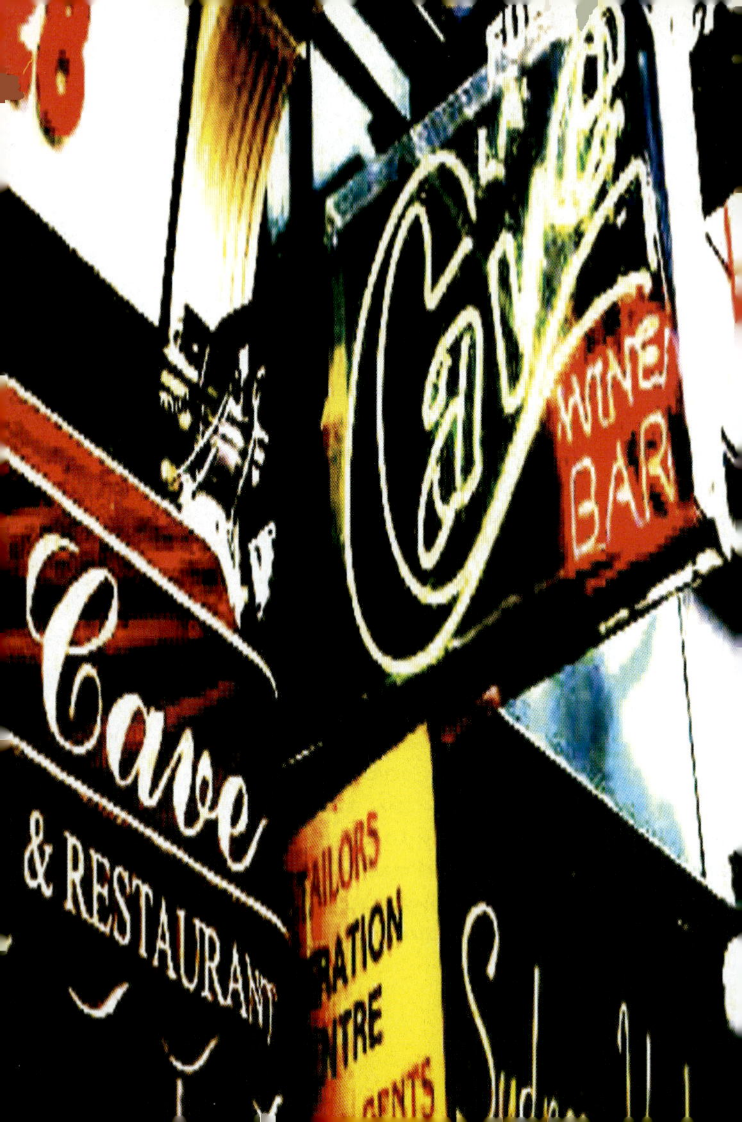
WINE BAR
Cave
& RESTAURANT

# La Cave
## South Anne Street

**46**

Dark, refined, vivid, classy. And that's just *inside* the glass. Outside, the same and more on a first adventuring into this intimate breath of Mediterranea which really does make a pleasant change from all that is busy and beery. Like a silver screen legend of old, La Cave is an example of how it might be done in smoky black and white fifties Nice and could well be the most civilised nightspot in Dublin. If there are any old Bogart characters still floating around, then here's where they'd most likely come out of the woodwork - all white-suited, cigarly gaited, fawning broad at their side - to induce, continue or end dramatically some fiery doomed affair. The rest of us can settle for mystery, that which oozes out of the soft-lit darkness and revel in the romantic potential that is born out of reckless abandon - the kind of which that can easily break the bank in here. Nevertheless, as they famously say, *you can't put a price on quality*, and I'd say La Cave's cellar knows nothing else.

JOHN KEHOE

# John Kehoe's
## South Anne Street

**47**

Okay – if Ireland's pubs are the best in Europe, and Dublin's the best in Ireland (*ok, this is just the author's opinion, before you complain – and remember, we're trying to make a living here*) then John Kehoe's could well be the best pub in the world. Already revered by many Dubs as their favourite city watering hole you just can't help but love this chapel of booze. Untouched by the sweeping changes the rest of Dublin has had to endure, this place is what time travel is all about. Go in sometime in the afternoon midweek, with the sunshine filling the dark and dusty front bar and imagine it's 1920. You could even bring a costume if you're insane enough – they won't mind. Honest. Anyway – this is it – the Holy Grail. No politics, no religion – the perfect pint and the kind of atmosphere you simply cannot replicate. John, I tip my hat to you. P.S. Please can I move in.

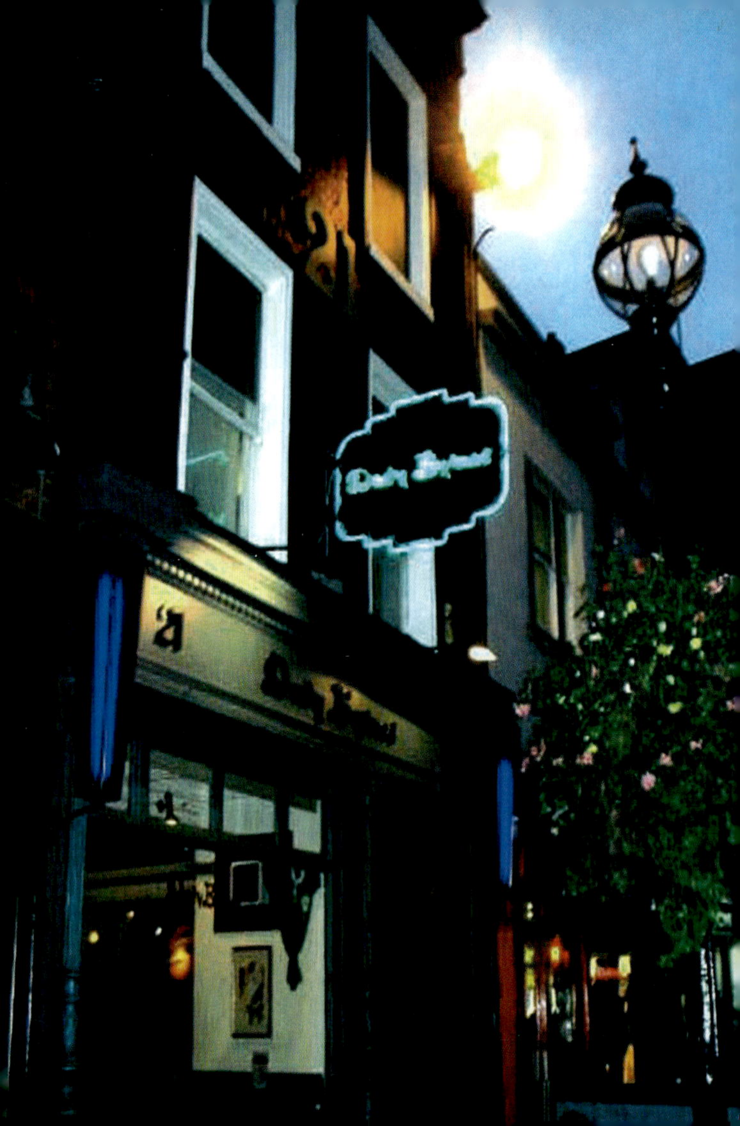

# Davy Byrne's
## Duke Street

**48**

Nice pub this. A veritable late-morning theatre of mastication and free-form devourance caused a thirst-worried Dublin man to wander upon wonder whether his requisite liquid measure might ever, under the sun, (I promise you), be ever proffered by the gentleman charged. Amid plate rattle and false-teeth prattling of Lord Boom Boom's latest land deal and Sunken Mary's fifth-time failure at succeeding in writing *The* Great Irish Novel, I really did have to ask myself, which part of 1904 I really was in and whether our dear departed Uncle James Aloysius would even cock his hat in such a hairdressing salon. I mean, and let us face the facts, how much blood can you draw from one old tome before singing from the sanctimonious sheet? These are the questions of the day and for effect, I requested something of ham to be mustered and the possibility of a nosey little shandygaff - French, you see, they like that sort of thing - but appeared to ring a note of discord beyond the said ramp. Strange that. Amoral, in fact. The pedantic ill-fits the romantic. Century A *or* Century B.

WINES

# The Duke
## Duke Street

**49**

*You can always get a seat in The Duke.* An ever-popular piece of Dublinese that, by virtue of it being perfectly correct, is soon to be taught in schools. And by virtue of *that*, your Social Sciences professor would certainly deem this boozer correct and indisputable regarding reliability. Imagine a lorry-load of art teachers and bookshop types plummeting headlong into a gaggle of office geese in some remote and cushioned hotel lobby. Well, that is the type of happy accident that will be filling all the other seats about you, should you be staying here for the long haul and is certainly the source of much *interesting* repartee come the witching hour. Despite the décor, there is a surprisingly youngish crowd in here, within falling distance of the popular nightclubs, which is perfect should you be suffering a little upholstery fatigue, but which also, remarkably, adds a sublime feeling of comfort beckoning you to stay for another.

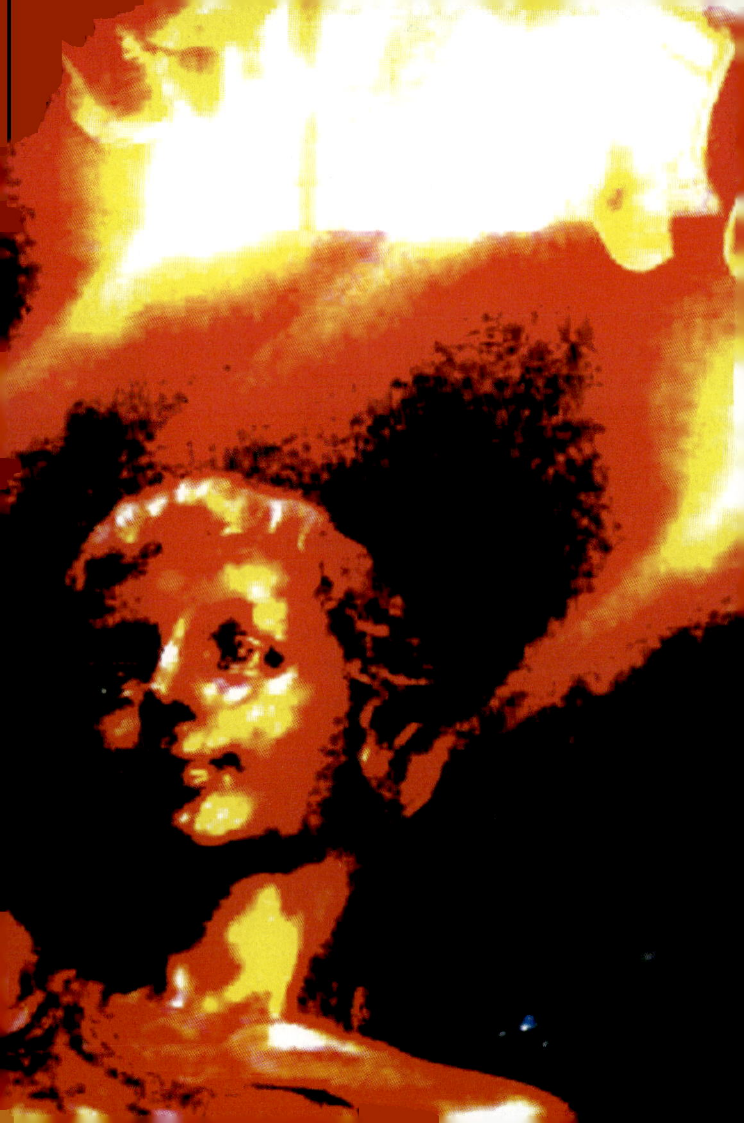

# Café en Seine — 50
## Dawson Street

Convivial, spontaneous chat for the hell of it, the warm creak of wit surrounding each perfect sip, the finest street philosophy known to modern man. The things, (however clichéd), known to burn through the veins of Dublin's perfect pubs so reassuringly strong and distinctive. But not here. Oh no. Most definitely not. The rise of this kind of multi-million Überpub has added a new dimension to Dublin drinking — the European idea of socialising as a form of entertainment. And these expansive galleries are the perfect vessel for empty heads and characterless jibber-jabber. *Blah, blah, blah, my job is sooooooooo interesting.* Really? Yes, I can see. Content aside, Café is certainly aesthetically pleasing on the afternoon eye, naked bronzed torsos and classical trimmings instil a gentle air of refinement, where you can enjoy good coffee and myriad cakes in reflective quiet. The clink of china cups and steaming froth machinery chime no differently to 1900 Budapest, and if that was the designer's intention, then a pat on the back is on his or her way.

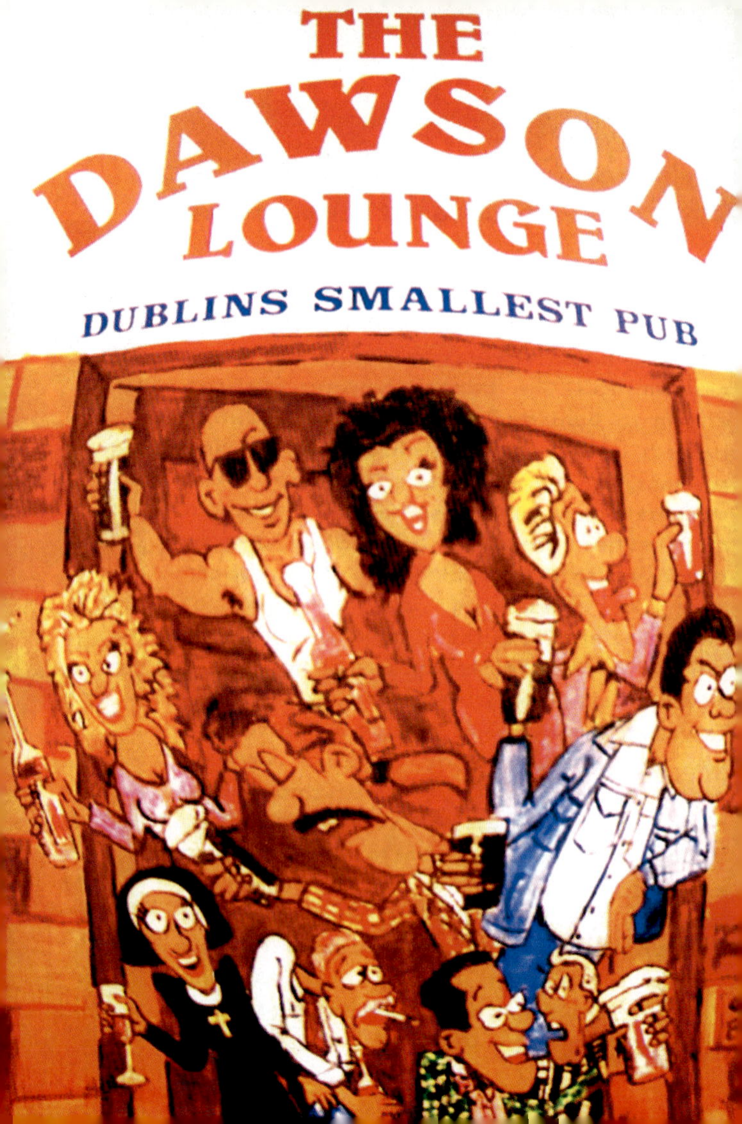
THE
DAWSON
LOUNGE
DUBLINS SMALLEST PUB

# Dawson Lounge
## Dawson Street

**51**

Imagine the kind of pub where *EVERYBODY* turns and looks at you when you walk in. (Think Clint Eastwood pushing through the saloon doors full of menace and intent). Well, here, where everyone is sat near the door (whether they like it or not) is exactly what happens. And, no, it's nothing to do with being vain or self-obsessed. It's just the way it is. Not that one should be intimidated, though, because amongst all the characterless, cavernous taverns that litter this particular avenue, this little lounge is thought of fondly by most Dubliners, purely for its novelty value but also for its genuine warmth. You can't really help it in such close quarters. As the original boozers face increasing competition, I propose that all good pub fans should support the *interesting* premises – obviously not all at once in this case.

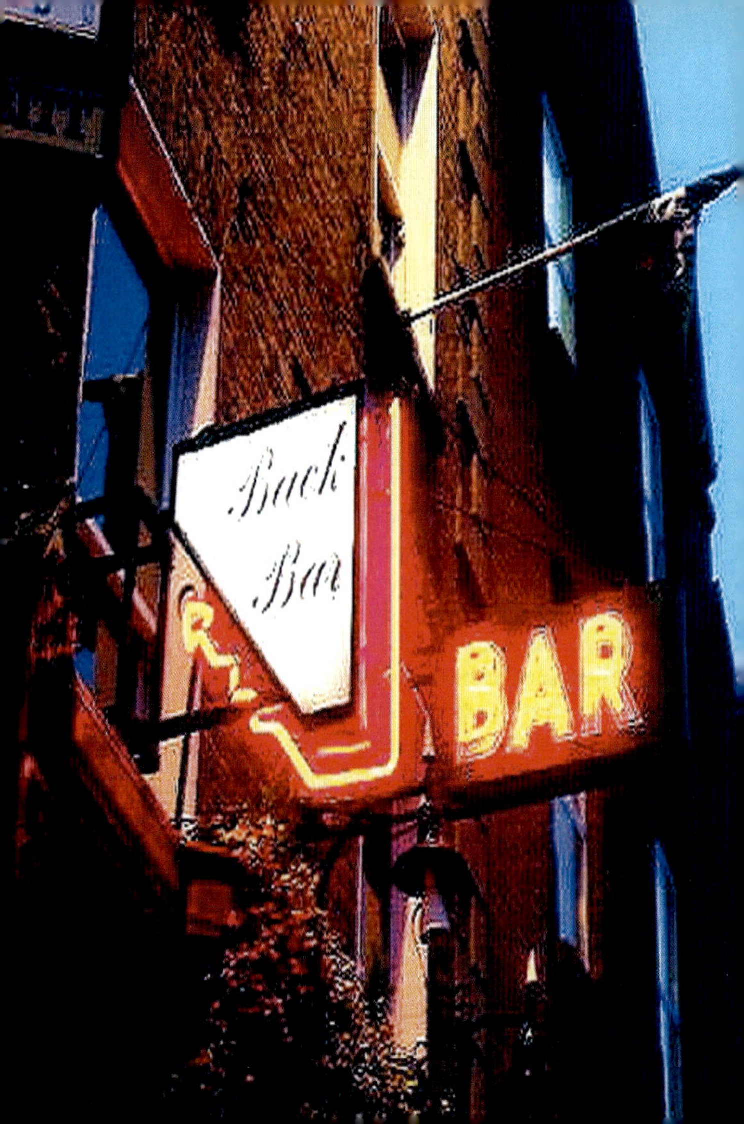
Back Bar
BAR

# Doheny & Nesbitt's 52
## Baggot Street Lower

The best thing about Doheny & Nesbitt's, and the thing that hits you straight away, is its dark and intimate, unmistakable quality. An original. Gloriously well-lived and gracious in age. If it were a woman, you might be tempted to marry her. Rich and reliable - *you heard it here first, ladies.* If, regrettably, you are otherwise engaged or otherwise inclined, I suggest a long-term affair. The snugs here are just the most inviting confessionals and timing it right can land you a prime rendezvous position for the evening. Afternoon, is wonderfully contemplative. But you know what they say, ..*every rose has its thorn*. And if you, like many, believe the pub is no place for religion or politics, then this lady is likely to rub you up the wrong way. Too much legal gavelling is enough to turn sour any inveterate pintman or wistful aesthete. That is what wine bars were invented for.

TONERS

A PUB

HARP

# Toner's
## Baggot Street Lower

**53**

Old wooden partitions under soft electric (almost gas) light really does it for me. The romance, the bohemian potential and indisputable past, bowing not self-assuredly in the grandeur of its simplicity. That's maybe what Yeats would have concocted had he stayed for more than one drinkee-poo on his (rumoured) first (and last) visit to a Dublin pub. Regrettably (for him) it was populated by repugnant common folk, those whom he claimed to represent. Unusual, that, and a little confusing - which is exactly what Toner's is not. The sign outside reads, *TONER'S - A PUB*. And what more information or motivation does any sane creature require. If you are only spending a short time in Dublin - that may be your downfall but, regardless - make sure that this is one of your spots of visitation. YOU OWE IT TO YOURSELF. This oozes of Dublin. The best of the city.

Toner's

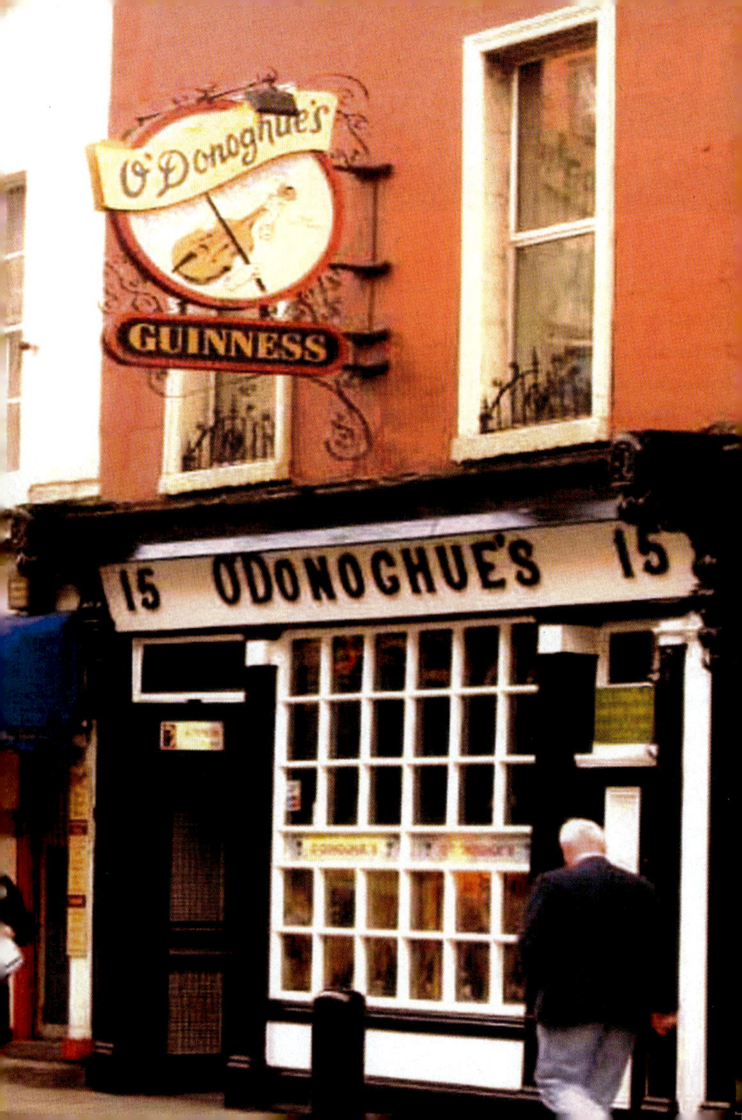
O'Donoghue's
GUINNESS
15 O'DONOGHUE'S 15

# O'Donoghue's
## Merrion Row

**54**

Now, when it comes to music, U2 would be the first in line to agree that the world-reverberating sound that grew here out of heady sixties sessioning, is the absolute definitive *sound* of Dublin. I mean, what an honour to have hosted such a profound birth - that of the brilliant Dubliners - and O'Donohue's certainly isn't going to let us forget it in a hurry. The bar is a shrine to its musical sons and the fine portraits of Messrs. Kelly, Drew, McKenna, Sheehan and Bourke are an attraction in themselves, especially to lovers of music. Forty years on, this pub is still known as the home of Trad. in Dublin and if that's what you want, then here should be your first port of call. O'Donohue's is lively but intimate, sometimes crowded but never uncomfortably so. Discuss the finer points of fiddling cadences with a bearded buff, grow your own and buy a bodhran and, most importantly, be prepared to burst into your best Ronnie Drew tones in spontaneous tribute at the drop of a hat. Toora-loora-laye, my children.

# Sinnott's Bar

# Sinnott's
## King Street South

**55**

Coming off the grey raining street and on down the solemn stairs, the explosion of light and furious clinking murmur of Sinnot's in full swing, is like entering some hidden otherworld. Well, Chicago to be precise. But what a sight! The final flight of stairs, the sea of heads, the city alight! You just want to dive in and join the melée. If you get a chance then grab one of the raised benches for a perfect overview, (if viewing is your thing), or hang at the bar and get a taste of Sinnot's cosmopolitan, international atmosphere. The Dublin pub experience (as a whole) can be a wide cornucopia of pleasures and winces and on the winces side, the only thing worse than a boozed-up gang of stag-night numbskulls, is a boozed-up gang of blabbering suits. *Raah. Raah. Faa-de-far. My battery's going, Jeremy..*Great. I like Sinnot's, but not at lunchtimes.

*Sinnott's*

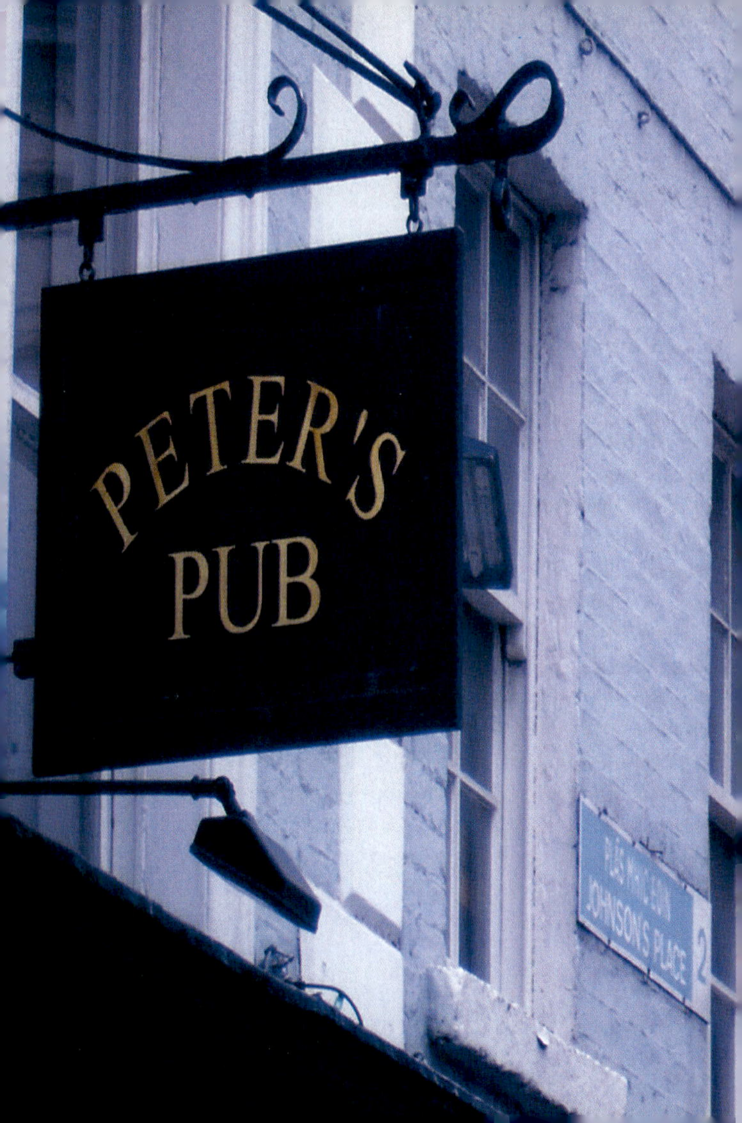
PETER'S
PUB
JOHNSON'S PLACE

# Peter's Pub
## Johnson's Place

**56**

Being a pubular person, I know many like-minded people who love great pubs and many of them say that Peter's is their number one. Sitting in its bright white light (redemptive?) calls to mind a cheery seaside café, perched high above the breaking ocean, humble and content with its function in the grand scheme of things. Peter's is refreshing and uplifting in its simplicity and I think it would truly be impossible to find this place offensive unless you were absolutely misanthropic and then being in a haven of conviviality would really not be a good idea now, would it? What does it for me, (and there's a moral here..), is the genuinely friendly demeanour of the staff. No gimmicks! No false American clown painted smiles! No pre-judging or sneering! Just, *How's it going there?* Plain, pure, perfect.

SK FOR
OLMA
MUS

# Hairy Lemon
## Stephen Street Lower

**57**

In a town famed for its music, it is a great shame and surprise to find out how few jukeboxes there actually are. I mean, whatever happened to personal choice? Don't people care what dirges they are forced to listen to on a night out? Well, I for one would much more enjoy a session with a few choice tunes and that is why I choose the Hairy Lemon. It was actually recommended to me by a friend who said if you like food, music and beer, then the Lemon's your only man (or words to that effect.) She was absolutely correct and for a while last year I was seriously considering having my mail redirected here, I was in it so much. Firing coins at Mr. Wurlitzer like a man possessed. The finest fruit-machine in the world. You can never lose! Lemon is a fun spot, with a good vibe and wouldn't be out of place in New York's East Village.

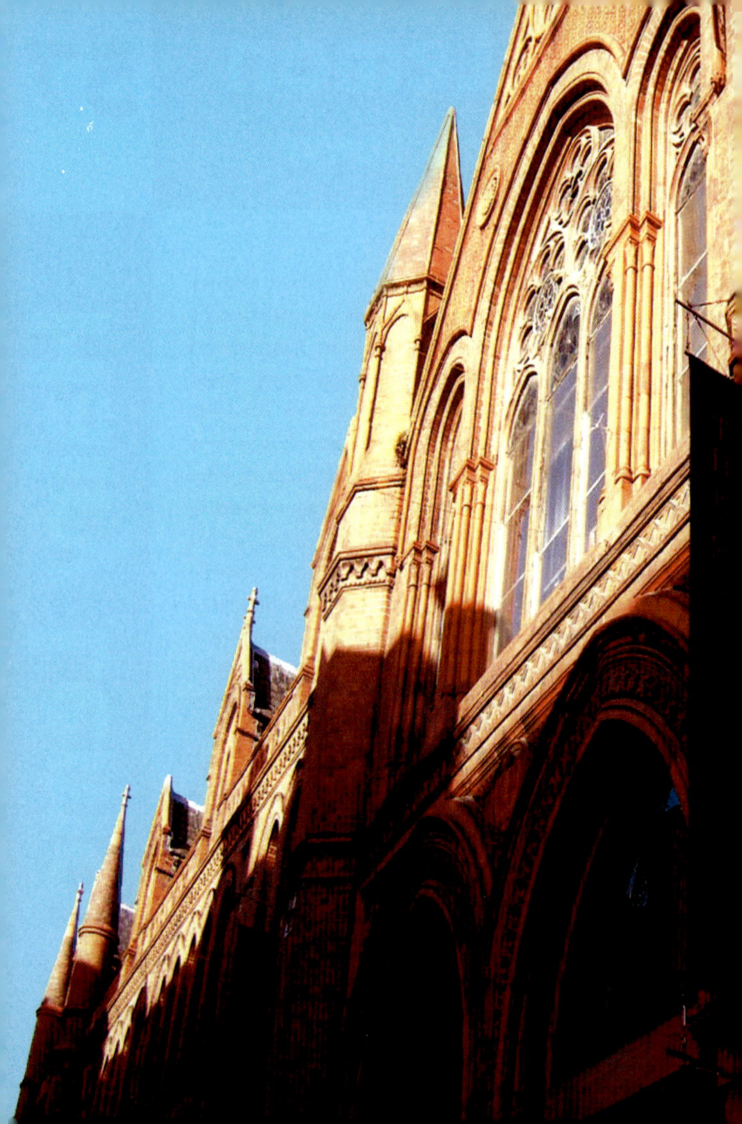

# Market Bar
## Fade Street

**58**

Have you ever been deep inside the middle of a dirty great cow shed, listening to ten thousand stained-glass bottles breaking about you? No!? Then what on earth have you been doing for the last fifteen years? Clearly not erratic meandering, but *hold no fear*! There is, insanely enough, an animated recontruction on the Friday Night Trail, humming somewhere between serenity and mechanization in a swirling whirlpool of air-kisses and feigned sanguine sentiments. Just what the darlings ordered apparently, if any night of theweek is anything to go by. On reflection, I guess this is the absolute antithesis of old-school Dublin boozers, hidden snugs and rows of creamy pints glistening menacingly under the familiar tick-tock. But who says that's not exactly what we need for a new and evolving city? Everybody and his sister seem to come here, and their friends seem to know it too, so there you go. If popular and trendy is your particular nosebag, this is ideal.

The Long Hall

# Long Hall
## Sth. Great George's St.

**59**

If you ever see an old photograph of a *Rare Auld Dublin Pub*, all 50's black and white and frayed at the edges, then <u>this</u> is where you may well see it recreated and actually still lived. A fading light of the grand old days of the turn of the century gaslit gin palaces. And although the manic murmur and vociferous clinking may well be lost to the sands of time, there are still living mourners here, pondering over pints, reverentially remembering the halcyon days of youth, excess and rumpustuous regular conviviality. With the slow consumption of every excellent and thoughtful pint, the silent (no need for words) eulogy reverberates to the unanimous and fondly recalled memory of reckless and healthless pursuit. Sadly missed, even in Dublin. Especially in Dublin.

**Long Hall**

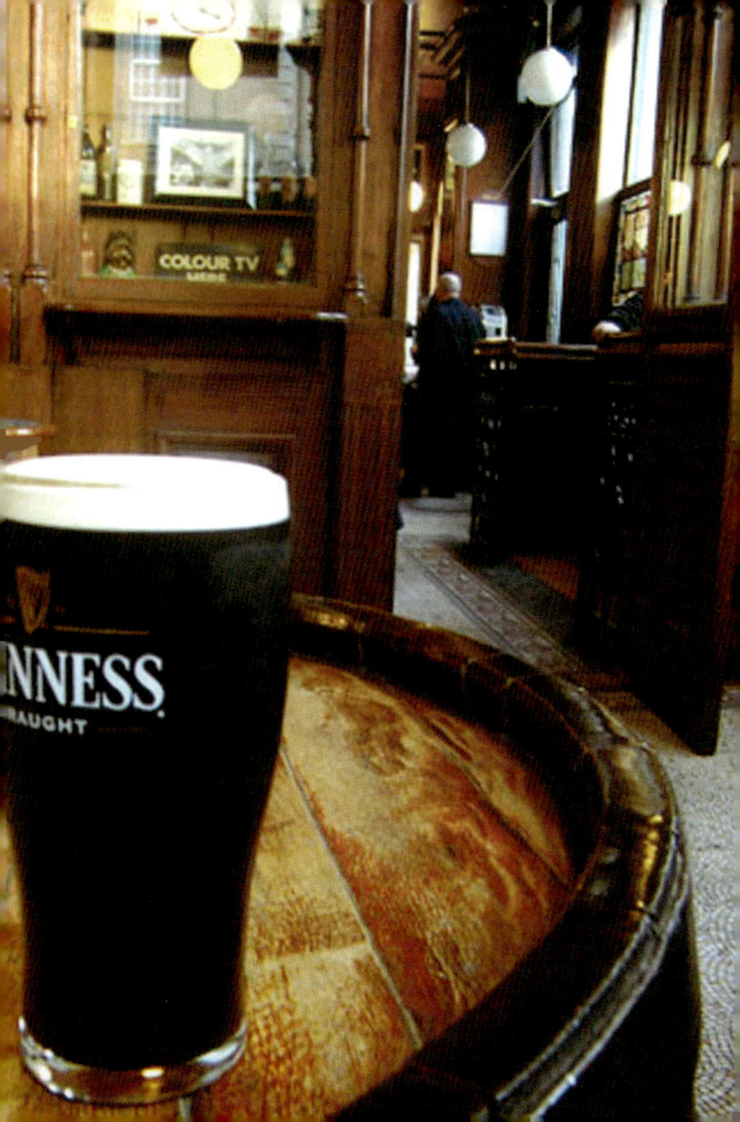
COLOUR TV
NNESS
RAUGHT

# The Swan
## Aungier Street

**60**

You know that old drawn-out saying about *books* and *covers* etc. etc.? Well, this open-minded hypocrite was sincerely (and deservedly) blown out of the water on this front. An utter revelation, is all I can surmise and God bless the genius who dragged me screaming into here. The Swan is as unformulated as it gets and the crowd as unpredictable as the surroundings. Pretty stained-glass swans, broken and ancient mosaics, clocks half-stopped, dusty and expired advertisements, reflections and deflections.If you ever wanted to make a time-capsule film about *all* of Dublin society at leisure, then this would have to be the location. In fact, go in with a simple camcorder and a spontaneous script and you are sure to have a blockbuster on your hands. (It might take fifty or sixty years but a blockbuster, I have no doubt). Anyway, back to the pub, (as I'm sure you're all growling)... The great thing about this place, as well as the brilliantly lazy barrel table with room for many, many pints, is the fact that it would survive in any area of Dublin with ease, and for one very good reason: **NO NONSENSE**.

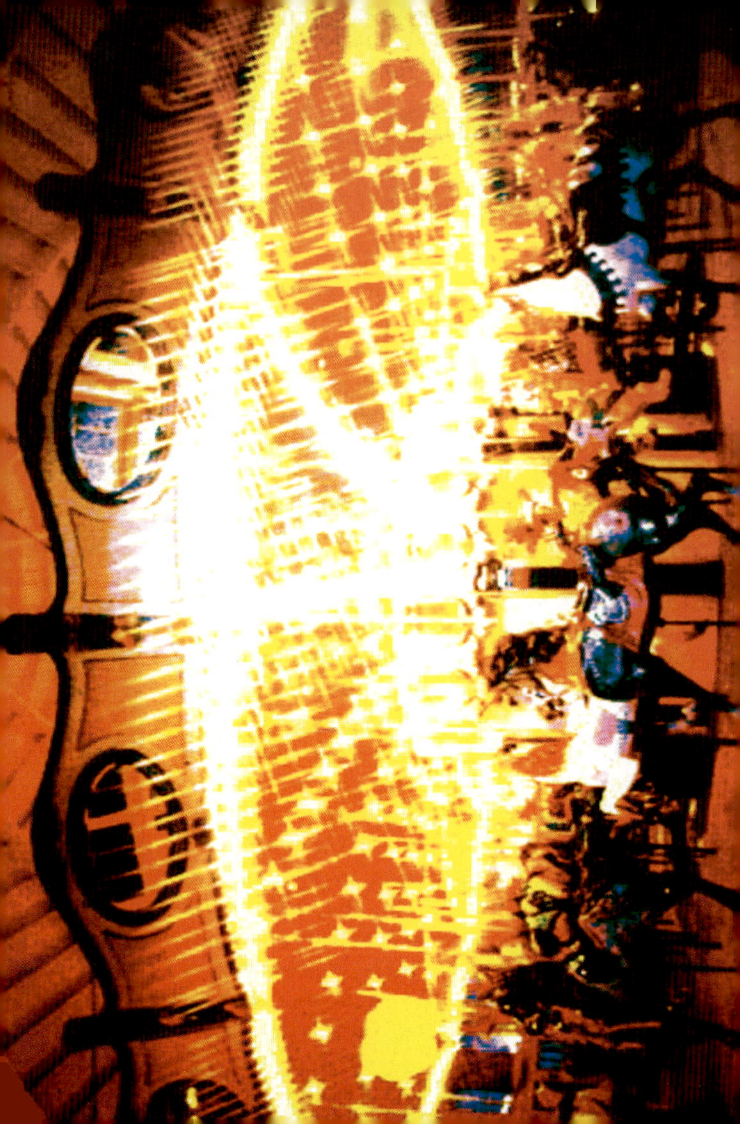

# Carnival
## Wexford Street

**61**

Young? Sexy? G.S.O.H.? W.L.T.M. similar? Need I say more? We all know in-spots can be as transitory and shallow as a sambuca glass but this here quiet contender has been limbering up gradually to take a worthy and hotly-contested pop at the crown of *Post-EVERYTHING Hotspot*. Effortlessly hip as hell and completely jammers come midnight, you certainly won't be having a gentle soak in here. You may, on the other hand, get a rake of rock'n'roll remixed and a shoulder rub with yer wan off the telly. Whatever floats your low-slung boat. Dublin is a small town and, believe me, if something or someone is happening or about to happen, then it is VERY likely that it'll be happening here - if not tonight, then VERY, very soon.

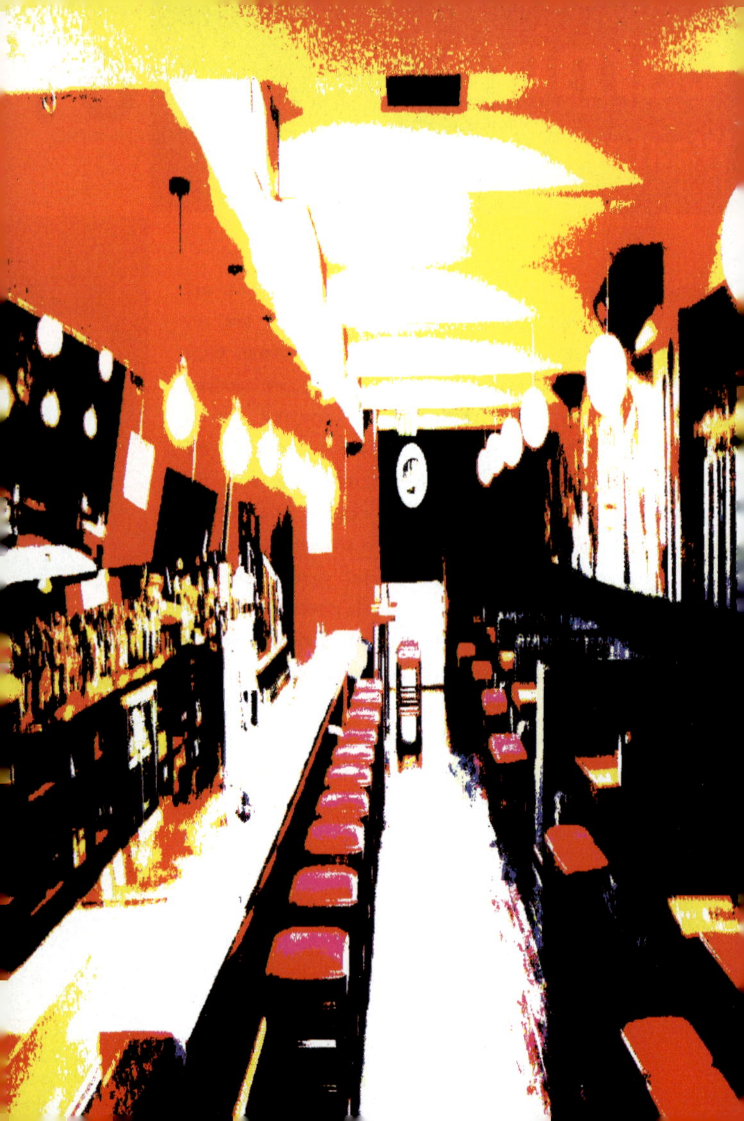

# Solas
## Wexford Street

**62**

Out of the very mixed bag that is the *new scene of Dublin bars*, Solas remains curiously attractive. Attractive in the *media-types - we could potentially fall in love with you chill-zone tone of suggestion* and curious in that, even though it presents itself almost like a nightclub, it is able to remain (successfully) open in the daytime. What does it for me are the *swallow-you-up* green booths which are the perfect location for "forgetting" you have to go back to work at lunchtime. Come night-time, when Wexford Street is buzzing with hair gel and handbags, this is the spot to see and be seen and with the Boogie Nights angled-mirror hiding nothing from nobody, there really are no excuses for pretending you are anything but famous. And in the same sense, remember that when you cast that longing glance to her in the lowcut top, everybody else will be watching - so make it good, Baby.

1894

WHELAN

# Whelan's
## Wexford Street

**63**

Lovely rock and roll Whelan's. Where would we be without you? I'll tell you – standing behind ten thousand other mugs watching stick figures on a stage half a mile away, having spent your weekly food budget for the privilege. Thank the Lord for Mr. Whelan. The minnows and the mighty of the rock and folk world grace this brilliant, intimate venue, which regularly showcases Dublin's up and coming finest, and it's also a pretty chilled out spot for a drink. Try early evening time, when the place is dark and bordello lit, making everyone look like a rock'n'roll star. Even the ones who aren't and never will be but congregate here for the music, Brother. Hendrix would approve. He told me in a swirly, purple dream.

# an poc fada

**upstairs at Devitts**

*Irish sessions nightly*

# Devitt's
## Camden Street

**64**

If you have never experienced the, (often brilliantly unpredictable), wealth of bars in this country outside of the capital, then this, (in my experience anyway), is what you may well encounter. What I am referring to, of course, is a.) good drink, b.) welcoming and warm atmosphere and c.) religious reverence to this nation's other two favourite pastimes - sport and music. You might be surprised, (and a little disappointed), to discover how rarely you will find a faithful home for traditional music in Dublin but throw ye not away yon banjos and fiddles for it grows wild and true in these parts, partly due, one would expect, to the wealth of non city-corrupted residents (the polite term for culchies). The upstairs ballad sessions are a must for the romantic, the rebel, the over-emotional and the homesick and might just move you significantly. Take it away, Jimmy, *Last night as I lay drea-ea-ming.....*

CASSIDY'S

WINE & BRAND

# Cassidy's
## Camden Street

**65**

Plush leather bar-room chatter and the bright sunrays refracting with dust, replacing the plumes of smoke of yesteryear, are my abiding thoughts on Cassidy's. Clearly, I was pissed out of my mind and shouldn't have been served but hey-ho, that's neither here nor there. What you do have here, is a nice old bar, countryish and popular, known as much for it's excellent window seats as it's visitations from ex-US Presidents. And no, for those who are half-cut reading this, I DO NOT mean willowing grey figures with top hats and beards passing through the big screen on the way to the jacks. Confused? Ask someone. So with digressions aside, it must be restated how good the window table is. I have known people to head in an hour or two earlier than anyone else, just so they could claim the throne for the whole night. Perfectly reasonable actions if you ask me, with the added bonus of the whole Camden Street circus to keep you entertained should the blether turn tepid.

*Cassidy's*

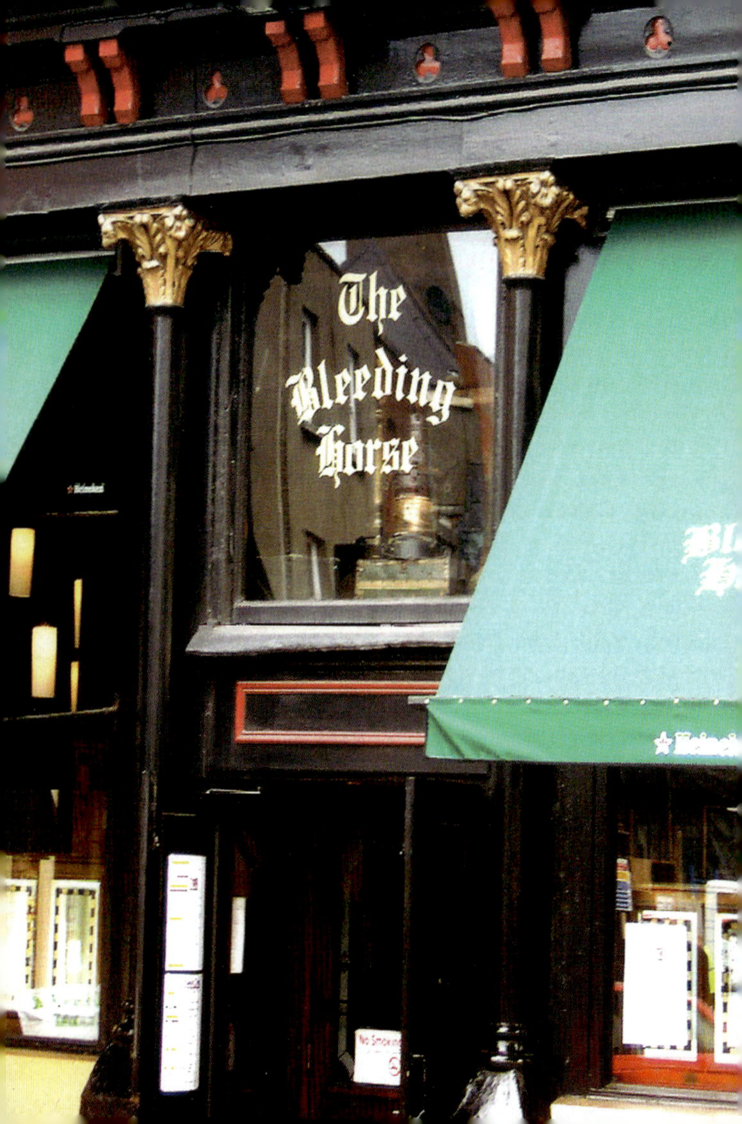
The
Bleeding
Horse

# Bleeding Horse
## Upper Camden Street

**66**

Previously an old coaching house, this is one of the city's oldest purveyors of ale and is possibly the most unusual pub on the planet. All wooden-beamed and horse-shoed, inside is a veracious warren of up and down bar rooms and wonderfully secluded gallery tables, ideal for conducting private affairs in the public sphere, as practised by generations of literary and political Irish greats. I am a big fan of goldfish bowl windows and the Bleeding Horse's huge panes are a perfect aid to wistful (or drunken) daydreaming. Watch all the facets of the Dublin day filing by, (and I don't just mean the traffic), while you patiently order your second or third and be grateful you're in here because you know all those passing would love to swap places with you. So, okay! If the name is not enough to tell you that this house is different, then try walking past mid-afternoon and I guarantee you will feel the magnetic pull. It's just one of those places. Get here early on the weekend unless you like standing.

J. O'CONNELL   29

# J. O'Connell's 67
## South Richmond Street

One of the most unique and appealing elements of spending a night at a pub in this country, is that, (if you're lucky), you'll end up drinking in the virtual front room of the local community. In the city, of course, would be the exception – you would think – until, that is, you step into O'Connell's. Here, granny drinks with grandson, nervous boy with his impending mother-in-law, businessman banters away at the bar trying to be heard, barely legal couple engage fastidiously in the far corner, the old boys gleefully watch the jumps on the telly. All manner of life is here and surely that's what it is all about. Nobody is out of place in O'Connell's unless you are grossly ill-mannered or a terminal messer whereupon you would be ceremoniously destroyed by the deadpan barman. Himself, one of life's tonics.

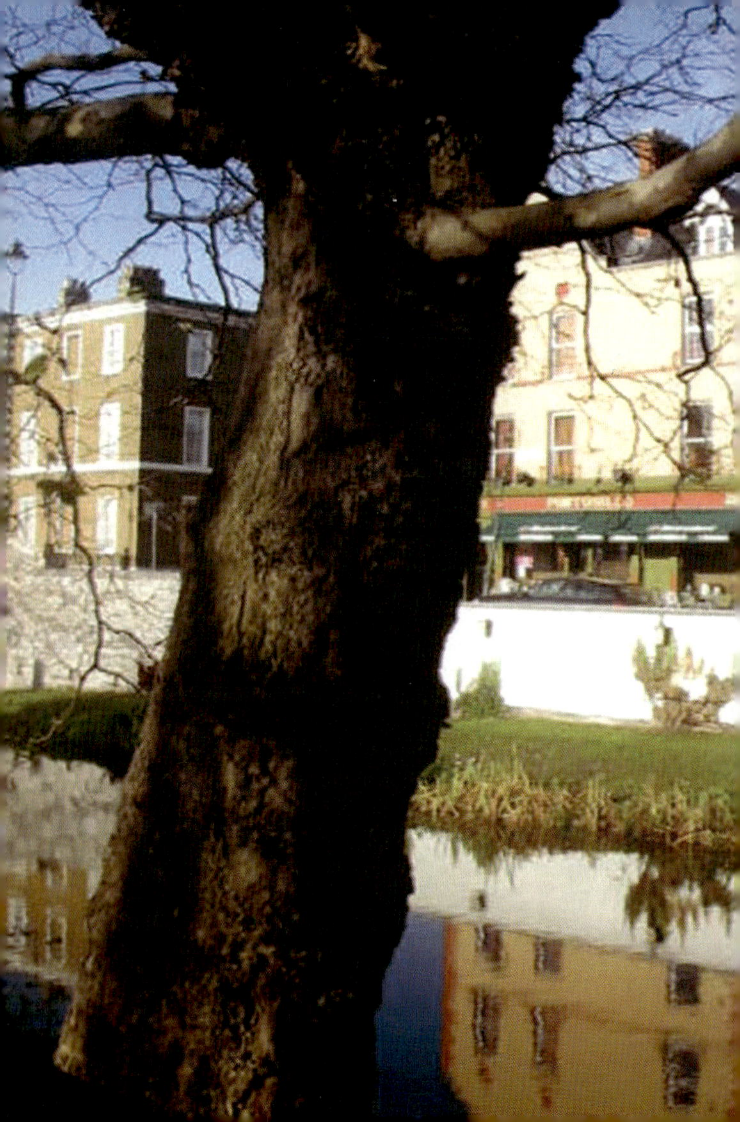

# Portobello
## South Richmond Street

**68**

Come on ya boy ya! Get up ya pup to the Porto for a pint! And other such boisterous hyperboles that one may wish to furnish one's repertoire with, should one be considering a few sauces on the Portobello's infamous Colours Night. No, it's not a political rally and I'm not sure it's got anything to do with sport to be perfectly honest, just the boozy county bantering that is funny for about five minutes. Anywhere which specifically encourages or invites a chiefly sporty crowd, unfortunately alienates many others who, basically, couldn't care less. Which is a shame, especially in such a picturesque pub which is just perfect for lazy summer pints watching the Grand Canal swans and saying, contently, Ah, this is the life! Deceptively magnified, the Portobello is a gregarious and, (dare I say it), fairly pumping house come sundown and the attached nightclub will keep you in alcopops 'til nearly sunrise. There's even a hotel at the back in case you can't be arsed to walk home.

**Portobello**

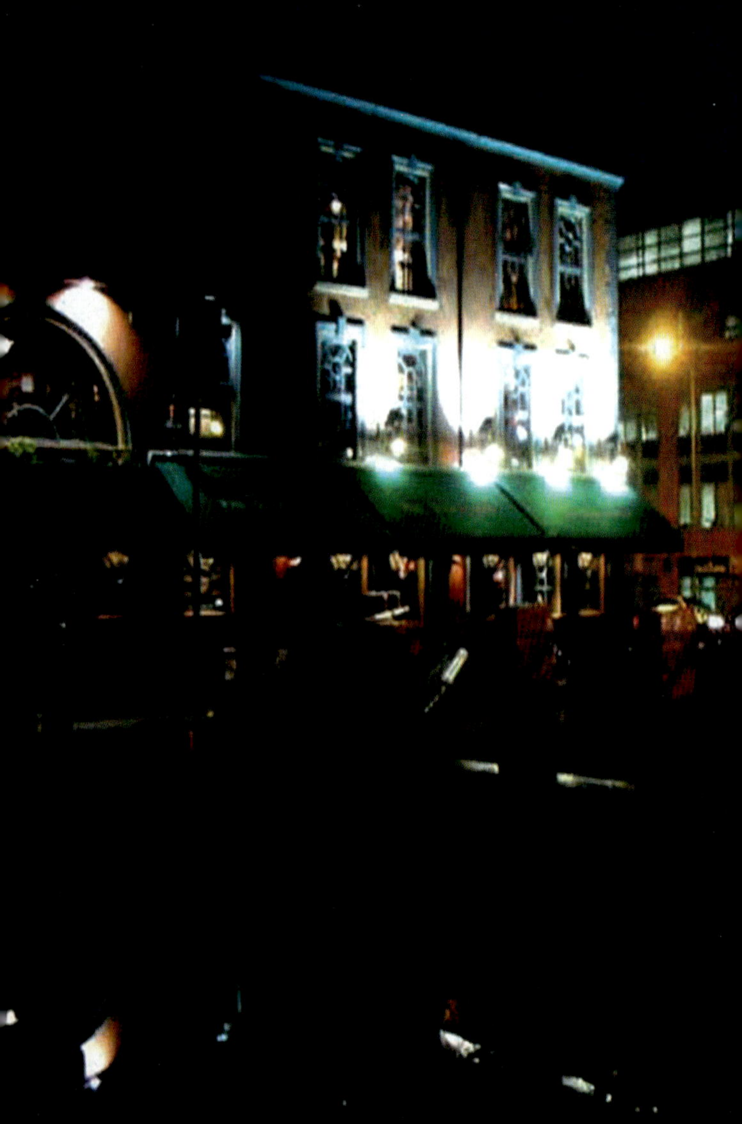

# The Barge
## Charlemont Street

**69**

Ah! Walking down the Grand Canal of a gentle summer's evening! Whether it is your special squeeze, thoughts and dreams or fifth can of cheap cider that you clutch onto fervently – this is surely one of Dublin's prettiest locations. So where better to spend an evening or lazy afternoon. Inside, The Barge is a strange amalgamation of different bars, seeming to be the union of an old house with a barn or boat-shed with an equally eclectic clientele. After promising myself not to whittle on needlessly about food (being a sworn connoisseur of *the other*), I truly believe The Barge deserves a mention on that front. The Sunday afternoon aromas from here will stick with you a long time. When the sun shines, the lock outside becomes an impromptu beer garden where you can indulge and be indulged whilst imagining Patrick Kavanagh's misanthropic ghost ambling grumpily by.

cordial thanks to:

Jan Farrell, Waldemar Werbel, Bernie Kearney, Michael Sullivan, Digiprint, Cici Kennedy, James Cuffe, Eoghan MacMathuna, Davey Moor, Conor Hackett, Eamon Phelan, Tony Hayes, Odhran Kelly, Puja Kataria, Charlotte Lary, Glen Keogh, Elaine Cunningham, Brian Wynne, Dan Fitzpatrick, Helen Webb, Don Rorke, Berg, Masa, Mattress, The Cats, Richie Curtis, Vince, PJ, Suzy & the brilliant S.

Lyrics on page 24 reprinted with the kind permission of their author, Mr. Steve Fanning ©2003, and as performed by Dublin's very own, *Porn Trauma*.

1. The Big Tree - Dorset St Lwr
2. The Woolshed - Parnell St
3. Patrick Conway's - Parnell St
4. The Parnell Mooney - Parnell St
5. The Flowing Tide - Lr Abbey St
6. The Oval - Middle Abbey St
7. Gin Palace - Middle Abbey St
8. The Lotts Café Bar - Lotts
9. Kiely's - Abbey St Upr
10. T.P. Smith's - Jervis St
11. Slattery's - Capel St
12. Jack Nealon's - Capel St
13. Sin É - Ormond Quay Upr
14. Voodoo Lounge - Arran Quay
15. Ryan's - Parkgate St
16. G.F. Handel's - Thomas Ct
17. Lord Edward - Christchurch Pl
18. The Brazen Head - Lwr Bridge St
19. Turk's Head - Parliament St
20. The Oak - Dame St
21. Brogan's - Dame St
22. IFI Bar - Eustace St
23. Ha'penny Bridge Inn - Wellington Quay
24. Eamon Doran's - Crown Alley
25. The Palace Bar - Fleet St
26. Bowe's - Fleet St
27. Doyle's - College St
28. The Long Stone - Townsend St
29. O'Neill's - Pearse St
30. O'Reilly's Late Bar - Luke St
31. Kennedy's - George's Quay
32. Mulligan's - Poolbeg St
33. Messrs. Maguire - Burgh Quay
34. The Bank - College Green
35. The Foggy Dew - Fownes St Upr
36. The Trinity Arch - Dame St
37. The Stag's Head - Dame Ct
38. The George - Sth Gt George's St
39. The Globe - Sth Gt George's St
40. Library Bar - Exchequer St
41. The International Bar - Wicklow St
42. Grogan's Castle Lounge - Sth William St
43. Neary's - Chatham St
44. McDaid's - Harry St
45. Bruxelles - Harry St
46. La Cave - Sth Anne St
47. John Kehoe's - Sth Anne St
48. Davy Byrne's - Duke St
49. The Duke - Duke St
50. Café en Seine - Dawson St
51. Dawson Lounge - Dawson St
52. Doheny & Nesbitt's - Baggot St Lwr
53. Toner's - Baggot St Lwr
54. O'Donoghue's - Merrion Row
55. Sinnot's - King St Sth
56. Peter's Pub - Johnson's Pl
57. Hairy Lemon - Stephen St Lwr
58. Market Bar - Fade St
59. The Long Hall - Sth Gt George's St
60. The Swan - Aungier St
61. Carnival - Wexford St
62. Solas - Wexford St
63. Whelan's - Wexford St
64. Devitt's - Camden St
65. Cassidy's - Camden St
66. The Bleeding Horse - Upr Camden St
67. J. O'Connell's - Sth Richmond St
68. Portobello - Sth Richmond St
69. The Barge Inn - Charlemont St

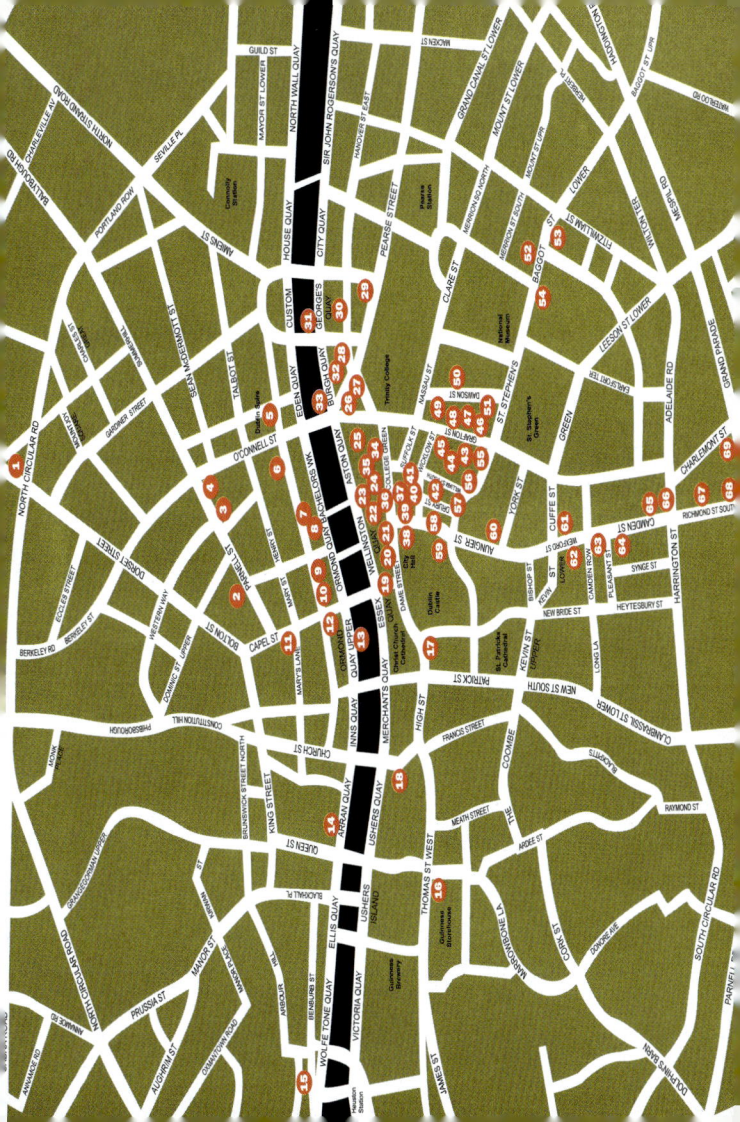

# Get excited...

There are a couple of things that get us excited at Digiprint.ie – great printing, great prices and great music. So that's why we're offering special discounted prices to DJs, promoters, bands and clubs. Here's a taster...

## Flyers

**2000 A6 flyers  €145**
(full colour 1 side printed on 170gsm gloss/silk)

**3000 A6 flyers  €245**
(full colour, b+w reverse printed on 170gsm gloss/silk)

**5000 A6 flyers  €345**
(full colour 2 sides printed on 170gsm gloss/silk)

## Posters

**A3 posters** (minimum 50)  **€1 each**
(full colour 1 side printed on 170gsm gloss/silk)

**A2 posters** (minimum 5)  **€15 each**
(full colour 1 side printed on 240gsm photo paper)

**A1 posters  €30 each**
(full colour 1 side printed on 240gsm photo paper)

## Cards

**2000 A6 postcards  €195**
(full colour 1 side printed on 300gsm gloss/silk card)

**1000 business cards  €149**
(full colour 2 sides printed on 350gsm silk card)

53 Rathgar Ave, Rathgar, Dublin
tel: 01 491 0150  fax: 01 498 184
email: msullivan@digiprint.ie

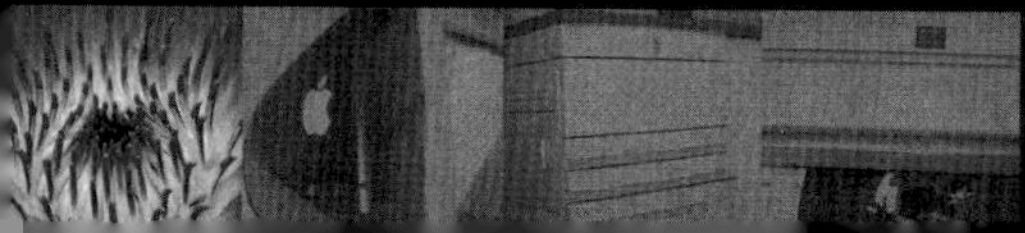

**digiprint.ie**
print & design